# PRAISE FOR DYING TO FIT IN

"I have read many accounts of near-death experiences, but the one that Erica McKenzie relates in *Dying To Fit In* is one of the most moving and profound I have ever encountered. Not only that, but the seemingly literal God-given wisdom that Erica shares with her readers is a gift beyond price. This book deserves, and I believe is destined, to reach the widest possible audience."

**—Kenneth Ring, Ph.D.** Author of *Lessons from the Light*.

"This is one book you won't want to miss! *Dying to Fit In* is an exceptionally beautiful and well-written book. Erica McKenzie's near-death experience is dramatic. Her dialogue with God exudes an abundance of wisdom with messages for all of us. With each turn of the page, you will find a treasure trove of awareness and inspiration. The powerful insights and understandings in this highly recommended book could change your life."

**—Jeffrey Long, M.D.**, Author of the New York Times bestselling *Evidence of the Afterlife: The Science of Near-Death Experiences*

"A moving, poignant, piece of work! Demystifying the Near-Death Experience! Erica McKenzie was able to take a most difficult subject and turn it into a compelling read that I recommend to all. Erica is walking her talk. Definitely a Must Read!"

**—Nadia McCaffrey**, Gold Star Mother & Child – Founder of Patrick McCaffrey Foundation – http://patrickmccaffreyfoundation.org/; http://www.veteransvillage.orgs

"The subject of near-death experiences should interest every person who seeks trustworthy credible insight about what happens when we die and the transcendent meaning underlying earthly existence. Erica McKenzie's powerful experience is one extraordinary case in point. It is a remarkable story from a remarkable woman. In a word, her book is magnificent, one worthy of the highest praise and recommendation. Expect to be inspired and enriched by this wonderful work."

—**John R. Audette, M.S.**, President, CEO & Co-Founder Eternea.org and Quantrek.org, Principal Founder, International Association for Near- Death Studies (IANDS.org),

"What Erica went through in the Psych Ward is literally an instruction manual for all near-death experiencers in how to survive what the medical community does not understand and refuses to acknowledge. Not only did she finally get her life back, she blossomed into an incredible intuitive visionary who now works for God."

—**P. M. H. Atwater, L.H.D.**, researcher of near-death states since 1978. Among her 11 books detailing her work is: *Dying to Know You: Proof of God in the Near-Death Experience.*

"This important book…has the potential to be a great contribution to the medical community and heal many lives!"

—**David Brownstein, M.D.** Medical Director for the Center of Holistic Medicine

# DYING
## TO FIT IN

**In Heaven,
God handed me a pair of glasses.
I put them on and then God said, "Now Look."**

ERICA MCKENZIE BSN, RN

with Virginia M. Hummel and Foreword by Dr. Rajiv Parti

ISBN-13: 978-1508840091

ISBN-10: 1508840091

Library of Congress Cataloguing-in-Publication Data

Certain names and identifying characteristics have been changed.

LCCN 2014959085

Editor: Virginia M. Hummel
Cover: Erica McKenzie and Sherwin Soy
Cover Model: Kameron McKenzie
Author Photo: Deb Ames

# CONTENTS

FOREWORD                          I

SETTING THE TABLE                 V

PROLOGUE                          XV

MY LEFT HAND                      1

TRYING TO FIT IN                  6

CONNECTING WITH

THE BOSS                          20

DESTINY OR DESIRE                 33

MY DARK SECRET                    38

ANGEL ON THE AIRCRAFT             50

THE FAITH CHOICE                  59

THERE 'S NO PLACE

LIKE HOME                         69

THE RIPPLING EFFECT               75

GIFTS FROM GOD                    77

A NEW EARTH                       80

THE GIFT                          86

THE EDGE OF HELL                91

BACK TO EARTH                   98

HELL ON EARTH                   104

I AM THE ROCK                   116

HEALTH IN THE BODY              128

HEALTH IN THE MIND              137

THE ADVOCATE                    153

HEALTH IN THE SPIRIT            167

THE POWER TO HEAL               182

COME TO THE TABLE               185

DR. BROWNSTEIN'S
        HOLISTIC  MEDICINE      187

ACKNOWLEDGMENTS                 188

ABOUT THE AUTHORS               192

This book is dedicated to those who are not yet able to see their value. With a humble heart I say,

*"You matter. You are important. You are unique. You are valuable and most of all You are loved!"*

# FOREWORD

I met Erica McKenzie, BSN, RN, at the Afterlife Conference in Portland, Oregon, and was delighted when she asked me to write the foreword to her book. I was truly touched by her story, her powerful relationship with God, and the messages she brought back from her trip to Heaven during her Near-Death Experience (NDE). Unfortunately, the medical community is reluctant to embrace the near-death experience as a real event or even discuss NDE's with their patients or their peers.

For eighteen years, I was the Chief of Anesthesiology at *Bakersfield's Heart Hospital* and specialized in cardiac anesthesiology. I am also the founder of the *Pain Management Institute of California*. On Christmas Eve 2010, I had a near-death experience that profoundly altered the course of my life. Following my NDE, I made a radical departure from my conventional medical training, abandoned my career, and now advocate a consciousness-based approach to healing. I also spend my time volunteering for community projects and teaching that chronic pain, addiction, and depression are "diseases of the soul."

When a patient describes a near-death experience, the most common reaction for a doctor is to dismiss it as a dream or hallucination. When Erica tried to share her NDE with her attending physician, she was medicated and committed to a psychiatric ward. As a nurse and patient, she was clearly able to see how broken our health care system was and the desperate need for training and education on the near-death experience and healing that included the body, mind, and spirit.

After my own near-death experience, I also realized the importance of educating doctors so they are receptive and supportive to the reports of NDEs by their patients. It has been a privilege to learn from Erica and I must admit that being in her presence, it is easy to feel the love. Her enthusiasm for helping others is contagious. She is truly a beautiful demonstration of the Rippling Effect and I am honored to collaborate with her, joining forces to bring awareness of the near-death experience to the health care industry and the importance of addressing all the components of the body, mind and spirit for healing. We are also part of a volunteer medical team serving Veterans through the organization Veterans Village (VeteransVillage.org), which supports Veterans, providing resources designed to help them to heal their lives. In the following true story, Erica describes her NDE in detail along with the lessons and messages she received from God. I would encourage you to read her story with an open heart and mind, as I am certain it will challenge some of your long-held beliefs about what happens when we die.

This is a story about gaining a deeper understanding of the knowledge and wisdom that God shared with Erica and wants us all to know and live by and it begins by loving ourselves the way God loves us. This revelation was a personal healing for Erica and the opportunity to help others discover and embrace their unique God-given blueprints and gifts. She realized that we are made to be different because it is God's plan.

What Erica revealed during her experience into *the other realm* is closely aligned with what I experienced during my own near-death experience in God's presence—God's *invaluable message of love*. Her powerful healing through God's unconditional love and wisdom serves as another humbling example that the power to heal ourselves lies within, and that we only have one job to do while on this Earth and that is to love. It is my hope that you thoroughly enjoy this book as much as I have.

Dr. Rajiv Parti

ERICA MCKENZIE

# SETTING THE TABLE

If I used human logic to make sense of the events I am about to share, I would miss the messages that Spirit graciously allowed me to be a part of during my near-death experience (NDE). In Heaven, God handed me a pair of glasses that enabled me to view things from His perspective. They came with great responsibility, and I am reminded of that each day since my return as events and experiences unfold around me.

God also asked me to be quiet and listen to the people He puts in my life, not just sometimes or when it's convenient, but always. I will be the first person to make it clear I am far from perfect. In fact, I'm embarrassed to admit that when I was in Heaven, I found myself arguing with God about my lack of perfection and qualifications needed to work for him. I quickly found out that God doesn't call the qualified; He qualifies the called.

Many of us feel lost and struggle to find direction and purpose in life. One of the most challenging things to learn on your Earthly Journey is to love your unique self, just as God made you. But what if I told you that doing this was single handedly the most crucial job we will ever have while we are here on this planet? Without it, we would be unable to fully access our blueprint, gifts, and truly fulfill our life's purpose.

How do I know? Prior to my NDE I spent many years wanting others to accept me and was convinced that changing myself to fit in was the answer. This sent me down a path where I made several poor choices that ultimately led to my death. I didn't realize that in my desperation to fit in, I wasn't changing the right things as I looked to mankind for my value instead of to God. It's been a struggle to learn to love and accept myself for who I am. I had become so lost that in the few moments before I died all I could think was, *Who am I?* I took my last breath without knowing the answer.

When you read some of the challenging life experiences I've had, good, bad and ugly, you may notice they all involve change, choices and secrets, revealing my flaws, imperfections and mistakes. As I reflect on the past forty-three years of my life, I realize these experiences were not mistakes, but opportunities for learning. They appeared as cancer, eating disorders, drug addiction, peer pressure, bullying, learning disabilities, endometriosis, early menopause, a career, being a parent, feeling judged and unaccepted, loneliness, heartache, anger, depression, challenging relationships, uncertainty, frustration, poor health, a near-death experience and more. At times, these experiences were overwhelming and I felt they were potential roadblocks.

From my near-death experience, I learned that these *potential roadblocks* were actually incredible learning opportunities and by embracing the lesson in each experience they would never manifest into roadblocks. Rather they presented an opportunity for me to choose to change something that would result in powerful healing and awakening in my life. But how was I to know how to embrace these lessons and begin to seek the right changes, when the choices I had made in the past, only lent themselves to change that brought unfavorable results?

Contrary to what I believed for the majority of my life, looking to others for my value and wondering what people thought about me was important. Conceivably, God should have struck me right then and there with a lightning bolt, labeled me a defect or marched me straight to Hell, but instead handed me those glasses, which I am forever grateful for because wearing them helped me catch myself and refuse to embrace those feelings, not letting them define me.

Looking to others for our value? How do we survive this messed up, unhealthy, non-productive way of thinking? It's simple, become the change. But be ever so careful not to confuse this with changing yourself because they are two completely different things, which I will explain in this book. Instead of stuffing in those feelings, now I acknowledge those feelings and use them as tools that help me to remember my responsibility to remain true to my unique self because I see things differently now. You see, if I do not live as my unique self, then I can't possibly love my unique self. Without loving my unique self, I would embrace my experiences and seek change differently. By doing so, I would be unable to fully access my uniqueness. I would not trade my uniqueness for anybody else's and believe me before this experience I would have thought feeling this way to be impossible.

People, I get it. I realize this probably sounds easier to do on paper than real-life but stay with me. Why do you think this book is called *Dying to Fit in*, instead of *This is How We Do it?* One, because unfortunately in my case, the choices I made were in effort to rid myself of my uniqueness in an attempt to "fit in" and it didn't shake out so well because it led to my death. Two, because ever since I died people have asked me all kinds of questions like, "Is it hard for you leave your dirty laundry in public for everyone to see? You must be embarrassed." and "Is it uncomfortable for you to admit that your imperfections and mistakes led to your death knowing others are going to judge you?" I can't answer for others, but in my case I am happily relived to report that it is not.

Dying taught me so many lessons. One of the most important things I learned from God was that *your uniqueness is your value and your value is your contribution on this Earthly Journey.* It doesn't matter who you are or who you aren't that right there should be a huge relief. If you are here on this planet, *you are valuable!*

I came to appreciate the significance of this knowledge for there were volumes of it contained within this single lesson. For the first time in my life I finally understood; My uniqueness is my value because it holds my unique blueprint and unique gifts that serve to truly fulfill my life's purpose. In fact, it is who I am and what it meant to be me. I was able to see the value of this lesson. I had been lost for the majority of my life so how then, you ask, could I ever discover my true self again and grow this love within me, when it felt like an impossible achievement to attain?

The mind is a powerful thing, and yet it fails in comparison to the knowledge found within our spiritual hearts. That knowledge is divine power. If we choose, we can unlock the answers by turning within and reconnecting to God through our hearts. I discovered it is through our connection with God that I remember who I am and it is through this connection that I am able to grow and nurture unconditional love for myself. By doing so, we can recognize and develop a connection with our Creator, fueled and sustained by unconditional love from Him.

This *Unconditional love is the key* to ignite the power within. When we seek that power within, we gain the knowledge needed to help us through every life experience, and as we step into our power, we reveal our blueprint and gifts. Our blueprint is unique just like you, which means no one else has one exactly the same. It is by design, the pattern that when followed; helps us to see that we are spiritual beings having a human experience, our sense of self, our identity and beyond the boundaries that may try to define our authentic life. It is also there we are able to see that we can overcome fundamental human limitations, and it was revealed to me that it is through our connection with God, that we can access them on an exceedingly profound level. It is there that we find the power and knowledge needed to overcome and heal from every change we face no matter how challenging or difficult. We can get through them, grow, and come out stronger because our blueprint contains the most vital information essential for us to fully embrace change and to attain total health and wellness by gaining the knowledge needed to help us heal from our challenging life experiences.

This blueprint holds the unique information necessary for us to create profound healing of our body, mind and spirit and identify, grow and use our unique gifts at the capacity and magnitude for which they were designed. We each have these unique gifts and these God-given gifts are incredibly powerful contributions on our Earthly Journey. To fully achieve their potential, we must use these gifts in conjunction with each other. It's only when we come to the table with our unique selves, whether it's the business table, the relationship table, or the dinner table, that we empower each other and can go on to do great things.

As I realized all of this, then it happened. In the winter of 2002, I surrendered and in doing so, I knew this meant that I could no longer look to others for my value and wonder what people think about me. Thank you, Jesus because quite frankly it's very time consuming! I had to refuse to let those feelings define me. In the face of change, I may not have all the answers but I don't have to look to others for approval and having feelings of uncertainty is actually... ok. I acknowledge those feelings, using them as tools that help me trust there is nothing I can't get through because I see things differently now. I have faith that God is at work in my life, and He has all the answers so I don't have to have them. It is a huge relief and comfort to let go and let God. It helps me to be free to focus on my responsibility, to be present for the changes that I am faced with, not trying to control but embrace them. At the same time, I remain true to and love my unique self, for it is there that I will find my value and that value is my contribution here on my Earthly journey.

My purpose is to learn. My mission is to serve. My heart is to love. My boss is God and my work is to be *me*.

I won't apologize for the childlike excitement, gratitude, and love I feel in my heart for my Creator. It fills up my soul and radiates throughout my entire being. It is the same energy that drives my excitement and dedication with more determination than ever to do the work I was sent back to do. I must remind myself to slow down, be quiet and listen, as I choose to embrace each day and the changes that come with it. I must be open to the learning opportunities that accompany it. I still have so much to learn so I must continue to do the inner work necessary to access that knowledge and continue to grow my connection to God.

People have asked me, "Why do you work so hard, try so hard, and care so much about others when most of them have no concern for you? You are only one person. You're crazy if you think you can change the world." My answer is, "Call me crazy but I see things differently. For as long as I'm here, I will be busy trying." Then I smile, reminded of my true Home and the time I spent there with God. What Dorothy from Kansas *(The Wizard of Oz)* said is true, "There's no place like Home."

While I did not get to stay in Heaven, God gave me the gift to see that the connection between Heaven and Earth is real. There is a bridge and each of us has the ability to access it. It is through our willingness to do the inner work that we're able to access and grow this bridge and our connection to God. Through it, we receive the knowledge and wisdom that ensure us these earthly experiences are all part of a larger picture and Divine plan. When we set the table with our unique selves, we can then work together and go on to do great things.

Maybe you bought this book in an attempt to fulfill a hope that you are not alone in feeling the way that you do. Please know that my mission is to serve. As I teach my message to the world, it is my hope to bring some light and love and knowledge to you, so you may feel and know that you are loved unconditionally the way you are meant to be – as your unique self. You are valuable and I can tell you for me, it is the driving factor in writing this book. I am only a rock (a vehicle) and if anything good can come from my story, remember, it doesn't come from me. All that I am comes from God, my creator.

ERICA MCKENZIE

ERICA MCKENZIE

# DYING

## TO FIT IN

ERICA MCKENZIE

# PROLOGUE

The pastor looked to me and asked, "Child, who are you?"

I couldn't answer. I couldn't even remember my name.

"Are you married? Do you have a family?"

I had absolutely no idea. I couldn't recall anything. I tried to draw a breath, but couldn't. I commanded my lungs to open and fill with air, but they wouldn't. I leapt from my chair and jumped up and down to force air into my lungs, but this time it didn't work.

In the distance, I could hear the paramedics coming down the hall. They might as well have been miles away because in that moment I knew it was too late. They could not save me.

*"Help me!"* I wanted to scream, but I had no breath to make the words. I was terrified. I was suffocating. *I knew at that very moment, I was going to die.*

The pastor was a strong man of substantial size. He sprung from his chair and pounded his fist on the desk. "Speak to me now because I can see it in your eyes. I know where you're going." His voice was fading. "Child! Do you believe in God?"

With the last ounce of energy I had in my body, I cried out, "I believe in God!" As I said those words, my soul separated from my physical body and I watched from above as my body collapsed to the floor below me.

ERICA MCKENZIE

# MY LEFT HAND

*"God hangs the greatest weights upon the smallest wires."*

Francis Bacon

The first memory I have of hearing God's voice was in kindergarten. I was five years old. My classmates and I sat at a slender wooden rectangular table as our teacher wheeled in a television on a rather large metal cart. She turned out the lights as the program began. The alphabet people danced across the screen.

When it was over, we picked up our pencils and began to practice writing the alphabet. Paying attention was usually hard for me and honestly, learning was a bit of a challenge too. As I studied the oversized lines on my paper, I thought about how to form my letters to make them appear like those on display on the wall of our classroom. I don't know why I cared but I liked the way the letters looked when they laid between those wide lines. They looked so perfect.

I found that I loved to do lots of things with my hands, from creating mud pies in my sandbox, to coloring for contests, assembling crafts, designing things, and most of all drawing. When it came to my artwork, I took much pride in it and couldn't wait to be rewarded for my hard work with a sticker or stamp of some sort from our teacher.

Of course, drawing included writing and I was determined to put pencil to paper and create my alphabet masterpiece. For some reason, I just knew I'd receive a special sticker that day.

Occasionally, I glanced up to see my teacher with her long, red hair that swung as she walked about the room.

Her voice was ever so gentle as she spoke words of encouragement and praise. She followed the conversation with each child with a stamp or sticker of approval for their accomplishment. I could hardly wait for her to get around to me. I continued to work diligently and peeked to my left, careful not to be noticed as I saw her approach.

She stopped just to my left side, but didn't speak. I thought she must be impressed by my penmanship or as she would say, "beautiful letters to paper." I tried to remain calm, but it was hard and a little wiggle of excitement escaped anyway.

I knew my letters were nearly perfect. I was sure I getting a wonderful stamp or sticker and the teacher was taking her time to decide which one would be most special. I finally glanced up at her.

"Erica, hold out your hands."

I placed my tiny hands together palms facing up. I was waiting, wondering, dreaming of my sticker when I felt a hard slap! The sting of the wooden ruler against my palms shot up my arms and brought tears to my eyes.

"Erica, we write with our right hand only."

I was stunned. My lower lip began to quiver and my faced flushed with humiliation. She had never done this before. In that very moment, I found myself thinking that not only did I write with my left hand and do it well, I did everything with my left hand. I threw a ball with my left hand, I ate with my left hand, played catch, and opened doors with my left hand. In fact, I did them so well with my left hand that my right hand didn't stand a chance.

Why was my left hand bad? I was confused. Why do I even have a left hand if it's bad? I glanced around the room at my classmates who had the same shocked look of disbelief on their faces. In addition, many of them also had a look of relief that they weren't the one being punished. At five years, I noticed something else. As I stared at their hands, most still holding their pencils, not one child held the pencil with their left hand like me. I hadn't noticed until that moment that I was different and I wondered why being different should even matter? I tried so hard not to cry, but I couldn't help it and a tear slid down my cheek anyway.

In a split second my heart filled with the pain of separation. I heard a voice. It didn't come from the kids sitting next to me and it certainly wasn't my teacher. I had never heard this strong, gentle, loving voice before.

The voice said, *"Erica, I made your left hand. I made you. You are of me and I am with you. I love your left hand and I love you."*

I glanced at my classmates and heard the voice again. *"I made their right hands. I made them and I love them too."*

At this point in time, I received the knowledge from the voice that we were all different, and it was okay. We were different because it was God's plan and it was important we knew that. I understood that God's plan was as natural as breathing and God's plan was beautiful.

I could feel myself surrounded by love and I knew it to be love because this overwhelming feeling was coming from my heart. It was familiar. I looked at my classmates and my heart swelled with love from God. It flowed through me to them and back to me. This love was a connection that I wanted to last forever.

There was no doubt in my mind that the voice was the voice of God. From that day forward, God and I were inseparable. God and I talked all day long. Everywhere I went, God would be there with me. I felt loved and protected by Him. I saw the world though God's eyes. I was filled with love for people and animals—for everyone.

My parents were religious and I attended Sunday school and catechism every Wednesday after school at the Lutheran church. We learned about God in this place and I learned about God in my home. My parents made God a regular member of our family. God was the one from whom all things came, and the Creator who loved me. I quickly grew my connection to Him.

There were three other people in my family besides myself: my mother, my father, and by the time I was seven, my sister. I called my mother "Mom," my father "Dad," and my sister, "Sarah." There was a name for every family member, as natural as brushing my teeth or tying my shoes. It just made sense that when God spoke to me that fateful day in kindergarten, I recognized Him instantly. I knew that voice to be the voice of God. After all, He was a family member too.

I realized it wasn't the name that mattered; it was the connection and the relationship with Him that was important. I knew God desired a relationship with each of us, as close as the one He and I shared. This set the tone for the next several years as to how I would see the world and the people in it. I saw the good in everyone. I knew at a very young age why God made animals. He told me so. Animals were sent here by God to help teach us the most important lesson— unconditional love.

Growing up in the small town of Arapahoe, Nebraska, with a population of one thousand people had its challenges.

Not only did I lead a sheltered life, the same kids who started in kindergarten with me graduated from my senior class.

As my grade school years passed, I continued to admire my peers for their uniqueness. I thought the smart kids were cool because learning was a challenge for me. I thought it would be so awesome to know the answers so easily as many of them did. I remember one student in particular – Shane Martin. I can't thank Shane enough for being one of those smart kids and never thinking twice when I tried to rub his head hoping some of his brains would rub off on me. If only "smarts" were contagious!

Instead of being jealous of his abilities, I admired them. I was quite thankful for them too. After all, Shane's gift came in handy many times as we both found ourselves in front of his television after school, watching the Flintstones, eating orange slices, and working on our homework. Shane was so smart; he'd already completed the final accuracy portion of our homework by the time I had started on question three of the same assignment. I knew God had given him his unique gift just as He had given me my left hand that could create so well.

I could see the gifts in everyone. There were pretty girls, handsome boys, and kids who were athletic. Some were talented singers, great listeners, others were quite comical, and some always had the right words to say in any situation. I could see their differences and God's hand in all of it. We were made to be different. That really was His plan. I truly believed being different was amazing, until one day in middle school when the cutting remarks and hurtful comments drowned out the voice of God.

# TRYING TO FIT IN

*"It's not easy to find happiness in ourselves, and it's not possible to find it anywhere else."*

Agnes Repplier

"**D**oesn't she look fat?" was a comment I heard more than once in my life. However, I never considered myself fat. In fact, it never occurred to me. I was 5'4 and 130 lbs. The truth was, I wasn't fat, but the beginning of middle school brought many negative changes into my life.

One of the less than desirable yet apparently highly entertaining aspects of my puberty experience was that I had matured early and therefore become a target for a few of my peers, especially the older girls. "Bush monster, Hairy Ape, Slut and Period Girl," were some of the names I was called.

Since at the time I had yet to receive my first kiss, I could easily dispel the slut title. The other titles were mostly self-explanatory. Thanks to my Italian genes, I had a thick head of hair with a natural wave that was hard to tame. Okay people, remember this was the 80's and big hair was in! Despite that fact, these mean kids still called me "bush monster." I took a mental note of the other girls and noticed how neatly their hair fell into place. I had the sinking realization that my hair was one more thing that kept me from fitting in with the rest of them.

Upon further inspection, I noticed the other girls didn't appear to be as hairy in other areas either. As I scanned my arms and legs, I observed the thick growth of dark coarse hairs and wondered how it was possible for three hairs to grow consistently from a single hair follicle. The kids noticed too and the result was the "hairy ape" nickname.

My tears finally convinced my mom to let me shave my legs. Looking back, I wished someone had suggested I shave my arms too. Maybe then, the kids would have asked me if my dad was the "milk man" instead of the "ape man." Had a Brazilian full body wax been available at the time, gym class would have been a much more pleasurable experience.

There was no doubt that I looked ridiculous being the only girl who had a daily excuse to avoid the girls' shower stall. That's correct. I said, "stall," singular, as in one big shower "arena" minus curtains or partitions.

*Were we cattle?*

It was humiliating enough that I was the only girl in gym class with a plethora of pubic hair and developed breasts. Privacy was nonexistent, so there I stood in the locker room, the only girl at that time wearing a Wonder Woman Bra or needing any bra for that matter.

I could feel the other girls' stares as they pranced around in the buff as if they were attending a naked tea party. Under their breath came the not so quiet comments.

"I wonder if she'll shower today. How do you like your tea? Sugar? One lump or two?"

"Are you kidding?" said another. "Clearly, she has two huge lumps, if you know what I mean."

"And that pubic hair! It's so gross. I'll take two lumps with my perfect life please."

"Hello, I can hear you," I said under my breath.

At the tender age of eleven, I blossomed into puberty and inherited a new friend—my period. And to really drive home the awkward humiliation of being the first in our class to get it, it arrived in the middle of math class while I was wearing white shorts. Several of the girls were thoughtful enough to remind me each day afterwards of that stinging embarrassment by calling me "Period Girl."

My periods were extremely painful and I experienced severe abdominal and low back cramps that brought me to my knees. Missing school for at least one day each month became a frequent occurrence. I was eventually diagnosed with Endometriosis. When I'd return to school following my absence, I'd hear the quiet whispers mixed with laughter drift down the hallways.

"Oh my God, look! It's Period Girl. She's back."

The constant bullying was taxing. One day, I stopped midway down the hall, turned and locked eyes with those girls in a full on stare and responded to their hurtful comments. "I can hear everything you guys are saying. I'm not dead you know." Although I pretended to be tougher than I let on, secretly I thought dying would be a hell of a lot less painful than facing their bulling each day and trying so hard to fit in.

In my desperation to fit in with the popular kids, I did the unthinkable. One day, after the teacher had assigned our class to work in small groups, she left the room. The mean comments immediately began from the kids in my small group. This time they directed their bullying at Katie. They made fun of the length of her pants.

"You have high waters on. Why do you wear pants that are too short?" they remarked.

Then one of the popular girls looked at me and in a loud voice and said, "Erica, look at Katie's God awful pants. Aren't they high waters?"

Caught off guard, I flushed in embarrassment and felt a fine sheen of sweat cover my forehead. This girl had issued a challenge and an opportunity to stand with "them" or against "them." I looked at Katie and thought *well they are rather short*. Suddenly, I found myself saying, "Yes, her pants are high waters."

Instantly, I regretted my words as tears welled and spilled down Katie's cheeks. In a split second, I realized the pain of being bullied was nothing like the remorse and shame I felt bullying someone else.

After all I had endured, I'd just inflicted the exact same torment on someone else. In my desperate attempt to fit in, I had allowed myself to stoop to the level of a cowardly bully. I rose from my chair to apologize to Katie but it was too late to undo my hurtful words and remove the pain and sadness from her face. The damage was done.

The teacher returned to the room and demanded to know what had occurred when she was out of the room. She turned to me and asked what happened because she assumed I would never be part of the problem. *But I had been.* I told her the truth of the events that had unfolded, including my participation.

There was only one solution to the problem: a visit to the principal's office. Back then, no one wanted to be sent to the principal's office. At the time, parents were able to give their consent for the principal to use discretionary punishment when disciplining.

Throughout my childhood, I had witnessed a variety of discretionary punishments at the hands of our principal. Among other things, kids were paddled, tied to their chair with jump ropes or had tissues stuffed in their mouths.

As I sat waiting with the other "guilty" kids, I tried to rationalize my behavior, hoping to take the focus off me and lessen my punishment. The principal's door finally opened and she approached us holding a bag of large safety pins. "Pin up your pants above your knees. We are going to be in a parade," she ordered.

We each took a handful of pins and began the task at hand. Once our pants were properly pinned, she lined us up single file and had us march down the hall in front of the rest of my middle school peers as she shouted repeatedly, "A flood is coming! Be prepared! A flood is coming.

I wasn't humiliated that day marching in front of the school with my pants pinned up. I was humiliated that I had intentionally hurt someone else. I have never forgotten that moment or the look of betrayal and pain on Katie's face.

Throughout the rest of our school years together, I made an effort to get to know Katie, the girl who loved grape flavored Hubba Bubba bubble gum. I don't know why her penchant for grape bubble gum stuck with me all these years but it has. She was also quite talented. It didn't matter what instrument she picked up in the music room, she played it beautifully. She never had to open a text book. She was brilliant and her singing voice was incredible! I was in awe of all of her gifts.

Instead of recognizing and celebrating Katie's talent, the other kids would comment on her weight, her clothes, or body odor. She was always the last to be chosen for anything. It seemed no one wanted to be her friend.

My heart hurt as I watched how the kids excluded her. Frankly, it made me angry that her peers were so insensitive and cruel. On occasion, she and I got together at my house and I taught her how to apply makeup and style her hair. During the makeover session in my bathroom, she sang the entire time. I felt as if I was listening to one of those female characters in the Disney movies, much like Cinderella or Sleeping Beauty. It was a shame that the others couldn't hear what I heard. They missed an opportunity to see how amazing Katie really was.

It's funny how I was never able to get an explanation about why many of the girls didn't like me, considering that they never took the time or interest to get to know me on a personal level. Several of them played a game where they'd pretend to be nice to me and then behind my back, usually within earshot, one of them would say something nasty. There were times I thought I was making headway with that crowd, but then they would purposely exclude me, and it hurt.

Maybe it was because they thought I was stupid. Many times in elementary school, the teacher pulled me from class to attend a special class for kids with learning disabilities. Though I wasn't diagnosed till after I had children on my own, I actually had ADD and dyslexia. Maybe my fellow students sensed that this made me different.

Or maybe it was my appearance and the extra hair that inspired them to be so vicious. I'd walk down the hallway and someone would pull the back of my hair or run into me on purpose just because they could.

Occasionally, I'd find a note in my locker threatening me. Some of them even called my house and when I answered the phone I'd hear, "We're coming for you. We're going to get you when no one is looking, drive you to the state line and tie you up to a headstone in the cemetery. We will shave your head and paint you purple." I guess growing up in the middle of nowhere encouraged the gift of a little mental creativity to dispel the boredom in many of my peers.

As time went on, I became accustomed to their treatment, but I could never get past the horrible feeling of watching them do it to someone else. Each time they did, I found myself replaying that day in middle school with Katie and how much I had hurt another human being with unkind words.

## *The New Kid in Town*

In a small country town, it was rare for a new kid to come to our school, so when it happened it was rather exciting. If the new kid happened to be in a class other than ours, it was a cause for extra celebration, especially if it was a boy, because the idea of dating one of our classmates was like dating a sibling.

When I was in sixth grade and eleven years old, a new kid came to school. Cliff Barr was the new kid in town and a grade above me. His curly black hair, sparkling green eyes and gorgeous smile made all the girls blush. He commanded our full attention with his quick sense of humor, and in no time at all, he was adopted into the popular group.

I didn't have any classes with him so I looked forward to recess when all of the classes congregated together. Normally, recess was potentially quite painful for me. But as the days went by, Cliff and I found more opportunities for small talk. Our small talk turned into daily conversation and the next thing I knew his friend approached me and asked if I liked Cliff. He said that Cliff liked me and wanted to know if I would be his girlfriend.

Are you kidding? I thought to myself, *does spaghetti love meatballs?* I was twelve years old and for the first time in my life, I felt good about myself. "Yes, yes most definitely yes!" I said. For the first time in a very long time, I was happy. I had something to look forward to at school and it felt wonderful to belong, even if it was to only one person. I felt as though I was making progress. Not only was he nice, but he was popular, and out of all the girls, he wanted me.

Since Cliff was in the popular group, I knew they had already accepted him and I was hoping that somehow they would accept me too. A few months passed without judgment from my peers and I started to believe that some of them were making an effort to be kind. Those few months were the highlight of my middle school experience. But it was not to last. Just as a few of the popular kids began to be nice, a rumor began to circulate.

A classmate pulled me aside one day and said, "Erica, have you heard that one of the popular girls likes Cliff? They like each other and want to start dating. I heard he's going to break up with you so that he can be with her. All the popular girls are encouraging this. In fact, I heard it's kinda like a game for them. If that's true, you know you don't stand a chance...right?"

Oh God, I couldn't breathe. My world folded in on me—a black nothingness. I couldn't form any thoughts. The words were lost as I was swallowed up in a tidal wave of pain and sadness and humiliation. Standing there frozen, I wanted to scream, "It can't be true!" After everything I'd endured in school, what a cruel twist of fate to have a brief moment of happiness stolen so unexpectedly. I'd thought Cliff and I were happy together.

The sound of the bell jolted me from my shock and I headed numbly to my locker. Waiting for me was Cliff's friend. He said bluntly, "Cliff wants to break up with you."

I forced the words from my mouth. "Is it true he likes a popular girl?"

The second bell rang. Cliff's friend didn't answer. He didn't have to – his eyes spoke volumes. It was a knife to my heart. The rumor was true. Thank God it was lunchtime and I happened to live across the street from the school. Humiliated, I just couldn't face the other kids. I couldn't face Cliff. I'd finally reached my breaking point. In a daze, I hurried home for lunch that day determined never to return.

My parents were at work and I was all alone. I never considered the possibility of ending my life. But I couldn't imagine going on, even though talking about ending my life and doing something about it seemed two very different things. Yet somehow that day I found myself in the bathroom. As I stood in front of the mirrored medicine cabinet, a young girl's face, riddled with pain, stared back at me. At that moment, I wanted to be anyone other than me.

I thought I could fit in and I'd tried so hard to do so. I believed I was stronger than I was, but the truth was I was weak. I didn't have an ounce of fight left in me. It was gone along with any hope I might have had. Now, I just wanted the pain to stop. The multitude of hurtful events from school swam before my eyes and in a desperate attempt to relieve the overwhelming pain I opened the cabinet door and reached for a bottle of pills. *Just line up the arrows and pop the lid off the top. It was so easy,* I thought to myself.

I poured as many pills in my hand as I could hold and filled a glass with water. Then I began to take the pills, swallowing them one by one until the entire bottle was all but gone. I went to my room and lay on my bed waiting and wanting to die.

I reached out to God and prayed as I waited for the inevitable. "Now I lay me down to sleep, I pray the Lord my soul to keep..." *I hope you can forgive me God because my strength is gone. I have nothing left inside and I am lost. I'm so tired, God. I am done.* "If I die before I wake, I pray the Lord my soul to take..." *I'm ready to go to Heaven now, even if it may only be for a moment.* "Amen." In the distance, I heard the school bell ring. Lunch and recess were over. It was time to go back to class.

Resolved to lay there until the end, I pressed my eyes shut and wondered if dying hurt as bad as living. Nothing could be more painful and hopeless than I felt right at that moment. But suddenly, I heard God's voice, "Get up and go to school. Go now!"

Something pulled me up and off my bed. I couldn't see anyone but the sound of that voice was enough to scare me right out the door. A dreadful sense of urgency encompassed me and I quickly ran across the street and into my classroom. The teacher started to lecture and my mind began to drift. I didn't experience the usual daydream sensation. This time I perceived the drifting sensation differently. I felt as though I was slipping away and the room began to spin. I asked my teacher if I could be excused to go to the nurse because I wasn't feeling well.

I stumbled down the hall into the bathroom of the nurse's office. I could barely keep my eyes open and wanted to fall asleep. I felt myself drifting further away from my body. In that moment, an unforeseen force came over me, planting me flat on the cold floor. I rested my head on the toilet seat and I watched my fingers repeatedly force their way down my throat. I started gagging and the urge to vomit followed.

I had consumed those pills on an empty stomach so as I began to vomit very little came up. Assuming I was finished, I lay my head on the toilet seat and the room began to spin once more. I drifted off, falling into a deeper sleep than before. Each time I did this, something would wake me from my rest and cause me to force my fingers down my throat. I repeated these steps until it felt like there was nothing left in my stomach.

I have no idea how long this went on but the next recollection I had is that I was on the couch next to the bathroom in the nurse's office. I confided to her what I had done. She called my mom and I was sent home for the rest of the day.

Mom had tried so hard to help me but I don't think she really knew how to go about it. I don't blame her. I didn't even know how to help myself, so after that day, we never spoke about it again. There was no one I could confide in who I would trust not to share my secrets. I didn't have a friend who had the courage to stand up for me against the bullies. My sister was seven years younger than I was. God love her, at the innocent age of six, she was busy having play dates with her stuffed animals and was hardly mature enough to understand what I was going through at school.

In my pre-teen world, that left my wiener dog, Snoopy, my parents, and then of course, Jesus and God. Snoopy definitely got props for his loyalty. He appeared to be a great listener. Between his daily naps, he always found a way to wag his tail and love me unconditionally. I learned a lot from my dog and I'll be forever grateful for his companionship.

My dad and I had a professional relationship that usually sounded something like this: "Hello Dad, what's the weather predicted to be today?"

"Mostly cloudy with a chance of rain," he replied. Then he would add, "So, how are your grades?"

"Oh good," I'd answer. At this point, I usually made a beeline for the other room because I knew if I stayed, our conversation would more than likely turn into a lecture of some sort about me needing to study more or work harder on my grades. My dad was a very hard worker and supported me in ways he knew best. I loved and I was forever grateful for him, but I was too embarrassed to confide in him about the struggles with my peers at school because I already felt I was a disappointment with my grades.

Thank goodness for my mom. I really loved and respected her. She was a positive role model and did her best to raise Sarah and me with love and support while working full time. After all, she had also experienced judgment from others when she found herself pregnant with me at age seventeen, so she knew a little of what I was going through. It was difficult for Mom to endure the stigma as a young mother, and she still struggles with that experience.

She became pregnant with me in 1971, around the time abortion first became legal. While abortion was an option, she chose instead to keep me. This was a courageous thing to do back then, but with the loving support and encouragement of her family, she made the difficult choice to keep me. And obviously, I'm so glad she did.

For that reason alone, my mother is my hero. To me, a great role model is not the person who traveled the easy road. Rather it is the person who takes the opportunity to learn from their choices and embrace the wisdom in that lesson. They pick themselves up and move forward. That day in 1971, my mother chose me. She chose to keep moving forward. Thank you, Mom, for having the courage to choose the more difficult road.

Marriage at a young age was challenging and when my parents divorced, my birth father, eighteen at the time, made the decision to give up his parental rights. My mom and grandparents raised me to their home in New Hampshire.

At three years old, my new dad adopted me and we moved to Arapahoe, Nebraska, to begin a new family life together. For many years, I was curious about my birth father. But out of respect for my adopted father, Mom asked that I wait until I was eighteen to contact him.

I complied with her request. I finally met my birth father while in college. He and his family were in favor of being reacquainted and wanted to include me in their lives, but I was just beginning my new life with my husband and raising children of my own. Timing and the geographical distance made it difficult to really spend time with them and grow these new interpersonal relationships.

In the years before I went to college, my family was supportive and loving. I was fortunate I didn't have the feelings of abandonment and rejection that many adoptive children experience. Yet, despite my supportive family life, the situation at school continued to deteriorate.

My mom always had a positive way of looking at a situation. I can still hear her say, "No matter what, I never want you to lose sight of how important it is to treat everyone the way you want to be treated, even if that person doesn't return your kindness." While I tried to practice her advice, eventually I told myself I knew the truth – that I just wasn't good enough.

I thought maybe if I was different than "me," maybe if I was beautiful, the popular girls would want to be my friend. So I tried to figure out what made them popular. I noticed they all wore the latest fashion. They had the latest hairstyles and makeup. But most of all, they were all skinny.

Mom tried her best to provide the latest fashions for me but it was impossible to keep up. Every now and then, I'd catch a glimpse of the popular girls staring at me. I thought they must like my outfit. Then I'd overhear one of them say, "Did you see what she's wearing? Who does she think she is? She's fat and just look at her hair...bush monster!" Their words cut so deeply. I held back the tears and pretended to ignore their remarks as I quickly walked past them.

I began to believe that "different" was a type of abnormal disease. You know, one of those contagious diseases that some people avoid catching while others couldn't avoid them. If this was truly the case, please God, someone tell me what the cure was! I couldn't figure it out. Even my mom's solution, that I treat others the way I'd want to be treated, seemed to be a mere Band-Aid and not the necessary prescription to rid myself of this thing called "being different."

Although I could hear my mother's words in my head, "Erica, I think you're beautiful and you have so much to offer, despite what others might say," I could see that it didn't matter nearly as much as having the right image. I began to notice how the fashionably dressed popular people were treated, even at church. These young women were beautiful and skinny. I know it doesn't seem possible, but they even seemed to have fewer "bad hair days" than I did.

*Ugh, God, this different thing is really for the birds.* In fact, I realized I wouldn't even wish it on the birds. Being different was painful for me and I perceived it as abnormal. I felt guilty because I didn't want anyone to suffer just because of the way I was feeling inside, especially my mom.

Besides, I could see how much her heart hurt to watch me go through the bullying and then later to have to help me with my endometriosis. I began to feel like a very high maintenance person. So I held back a lot from my mom in hopes of sparing her from more unnecessary hurt. As a result, the only one I felt I could turn to was God.

# CONNECTING WITH THE BOSS

*"What no eye has seen, nor ear heard, nor the heart of man imagined, what God has prepared for those who love him — these things God has revealed to us through the Spirit."*

1 Corinthians 2:9 (ESV)

The eventful days at school were usually followed by heated conversations with the Boss at bedtime, which went something like this: "Our Father, Who art in Heaven, hallowed be thy name." *Seriously? I have to be honest God, since you can already read my mind. I want you to know that I used to be terrified and thought the worst possible, most terrible thing would be to die. I mean, let's be honest. I'm a sinner, not a winner. I don't really know how else to put it, and although I feel like I'm going through Hell right now, I don't want to go to the Hell that the pastor talks about in church. I can't begin to wrap my head around the concept of knowing that once we die, it's forever.*

"Thy Kingdom come, thy will be done," I said aloud as I continued the Lord's Prayer and my regular conversation with God.

*Don't get me wrong God. A part of me can't wait to go to Heaven, even if it's only for a moment until you judge me. I often daydream while I'm in church, listening to the sermon. Again, I'm so sorry God. I know I should be paying attention to your words, but lately, I find my mind wanders and it goes to a place where I visualize what it's really like in Heaven. I mean, do people really sit around playing harps all day and singing to you?*

*Do you have such a thing as Heaven School? Gosh, if there is, please tell me we don't have to study. How hard is it, really God, to fit in up in Heaven? Is there a pecking order? Are there popular groups up there as well?*

"Give us this day our daily bread and forgive us our trespasses."

*Clearly, I'm not perfect, as I'm reminded on a daily basis. The pastor has made it clear that I am a sinner and you will judge me someday. I guess I deserve it. I guess I deserve judgment from others too.*

"As we forgive those who trespass against us. And lead us not into temptation but deliver us from evil."

*I just wish I could make it better, God. I wish with all my heart that I could figure out a way to end this terrible awful meanness. I'm a reasonable person so I'll make you a deal. If you help me, then I promise I will try my best to help put an end to the awful meanness in the world.*

"For thine is the kingdom and the power."

*Which reminds me, God, if you could spare a little power, please send someone with a cure right away as I seem to have caught a bad case of "the abnormal different." I could really use the extra strength right now to help me fight this disease. As you know God, I'm trying to fit in.*

Unfortunately, one day seemed to blend into another and I still longed to fit in and be a part of the popular group. There were times it appeared I was making headway. Then they would purposely exclude me, and it hurt.

As I look back now, it's easy to see that I shouldn't have wanted to be part of such a group, but back then we all wanted to be included in the popular group, to fit in. We didn't want to be different. I could never understand what I'd done wrong or why I wasn't accepted as part of their group.

I still wondered if maybe they thought I was stupid because I had to attend a special class for learning disabilities. When they pulled my hair or ran into me on purpose, I didn't know how to react. I guess for many of my peers, growing up in the middle of nowhere encouraged mental creativity in order to dispel their boredom.

I just couldn't understand their behavior and why they felt it was necessary to be so hurtful. The "fake nice" and gossip that ran rampant with many of them was also difficult to comprehend. Yet at twelve, it seemed more important to be like them than to be different.

It seemed that overnight the majority of the children who had once loved and accepted each other became cruel and judgmental. It was hard to ignore their stinging comments. I spent countless nights crying to my mom and praying to God to help the kids to be nice to me.

One day after school, Mom mentioned she thought the girls were mean to me because I was beautiful and they were jealous. But I thought all the girls who made fun of me were so beautiful. It didn't make sense. How could thinking someone was beautiful be attached to a negative response? I was confused and truly didn't know what to think. One thing was clear though – I knew I couldn't really be beautiful because the gift of beauty came from God. How could a gift that He created produce such a negative reaction from other human beings?

I had already experienced my kindergarten teacher's reaction to the use of my left hand for my schoolwork. The combination of that experience and being harassed by the mean kids who made fun of me was overwhelming. Obviously, if my schoolmates were reacting so negatively towards me, it must mean that I was not really beautiful and my mother was wrong. That very night in seventh grade, I made a decision to become this thing they called *beautiful*. I just knew in my heart that *this was the cure that was needed to rid me of the abnormal difference once and for all.* When I eventually got there, all the peers in my school would finally accept me.

Now when I reflect back on my experiences, I wish I had developed the courage to reach out to my teachers for help. But back then, I was afraid of being labeled a tattletale. I can see now how it was all so superficial and petty. As a young girl, I didn't have the wisdom to know how to really love, value, and advocate for myself. I wanted so badly for people to like me, but it seemed the harder I tried the worse their reactions became.

One day a little voice inside of me said *it doesn't have to be this way.* I was passing between classes and I remember looking around and taking a mental note of all of the popular girls in the hallway. The lights went on and that's when I made a beeline to the girl's bathroom.

I did a quick scan to see if there were any feet showing in the stalls. The bathroom was empty. I was alone. This was different from the feeling of being alone I experienced when I stood in the midst of a group and experienced loneliness down to my bones. This *alone* had power. I was in control.

Quickly, I made my way to the last bathroom stall and locked the door. I lifted the lid of the toilet and stuck two fingers of my left hand down my throat. My eyes watered and I coughed twice. I forced my fingers down my throat again, this time with urgency, purpose, and determination. My partially eaten lunch landed in the toilet.

With each purge came an incredible sense of relief. I was in control. I was finally at peace. There in the last stall of the girl's bathroom, I found a place where I could escape the "old" me.

Had I finally found the cure? Was this the magic prescription to rid me of the curse of being different once and for all? I glanced at my stomach and noticed a trickle of vomit on my new outfit—a hot pink one piece overall. Suddenly, I was ashamed. It was the outfit I wasn't supposed to have at all because it put me over my one new outfit per month limit.

In the case of this pink overall set, my mom had made an exception and this was outfit number two for the month. It was a big sacrifice for her in an attempt to help me fit in so the negative comments would happen less. As I look back now, I can see how much she tried to help ease my pain and I am so grateful for her love and support through the years.

But now, thanks to my bulimia, I could literally purge the loneliness and heartache I felt. I was in control of my destiny. It didn't stop the gossip from the girls, their "fake nice" or their cruel comments, but it allowed me a way to relieve the pain and frustration inside without taking it out on others. I was finally making progress.

Pouring myself into creating the new me, I joined every team and club I could, including volleyball, basketball, track and cheerleading. I was unstoppable. I enrolled in all these activities starting in 7th grade and added more when I went to high school. Somehow, I had hoped high school would be different, that because I was involved in so many things, I would be accepted. But it turned out to be more of the same, including my bulimia.

Once again, I found myself doing what I did best. I filled every waking moment with activity. I continued with volleyball, basketball and track, and added editor of the school newspaper, yearbook staff and captain of the cheerleading squad, marching band, jazz band, drum major, class plays, musicals, Future Homemakers of America, and a youth group. Somewhere in there I also managed to fit in my studies.

One of the few advantages of living in a small town, with a small school, was that many of the student body found they needed to participate in multiple activities because there just weren't enough people to fill the rosters and clubs if they didn't. Participating would put me in a position to be with a majority of my peers at different times, and this would give me the ability to include people in the groups as opposed to excluding them.

I even managed to have a best friend, which definitely helped me to survive my high school years. Looking back, I can honestly say that I really enjoyed participating in so many activities and I developed the gift of multitasking on a big level. However, one thing did remain the same; most of the popular girls and some of my peers, continued to be "fake nice" to my face and hurtful within earshot.

## Seeing Spirit

Nevertheless, there was another reason that added to my feeling of being different, separate from the rest of my peers. I couldn't tell a soul because I knew my secret would make things at school that much worse.

I remember the first time I noticed that I had what seemed to be a very unique ability. I had just turned old enough to stay at home by myself while my parents were at work. My sister, Sarah, who was seven years younger, must have been at daycare. I had just returned from swimming all day, something I loved to do and one of the few things available in a small town to keep kids busy.

As I sat at the kitchen table, still wrapped in my damp towel and swimsuit, I noticed the new phone book had arrived. It was sitting on the table in front of me and I randomly flipped it open to the middle of the yellow pages. As I stared at the pages, the oddest thought came to mind, to see if I could make them turn without touching them. I don't know where that thought came from but I had the strongest urge to try it.

Staring at the pages, I thought, *I can make my mind move this page.* Suddenly, the page turned by itself...*Just one page.* I was dumfounded as I glanced around the room and realized there was no wind, no fan, nothing that might explain what had just happened.

I was so excited and I wanted to tell somebody. But sadly, I became conscious of the fact that I couldn't share this with anyone. Whenever I shared such incidents with them, my parents brushed off such experiences as figments of my imagination. Yet, somehow, turning the page of the phonebook with my mind seemed like a natural thing for me to do. Even though I couldn't explain it, I would never forget what had just happened...ever.

Starting at a very young age, I also had the ability to see Spirit. I was convinced that my house was haunted. It was a very old house and at one time, a doctor and his family had lived there. I told my mother he used to see many sick patients there and, in fact, there were many people who died in the house and hadn't left. Mom said to the best of her knowledge, the doctor never saw his patients at the house. But I knew better.

There was a period during my childhood when different spirits who had crossed over came to visit me. They seemed to prefer to come at night when I was alone in my bed. I would usually awake from sleeping, sit up and open my eyes, and there standing or sitting at the end of my bed would be someone in spirit form.

Even though there were many different spirits, I only knew some of their identities. I recognized them as loved ones who had crossed over, but I didn't know their names. Some spirits took on a human form and others took on a form I didn't recognize. I had the knowledge that those were never of this world. However, there were a few patterns I was soon able to identify that linked them all together. They all communicated the same way. Even though I didn't have a name for this way of communicating as a child, by adulthood I would learn that it was called telepathic communication.

In addition, it didn't matter who or what came to me, even though almost every time my initial response was sheer terror. I had a sense that none of them ever wanted to harm me and none of them were negative. Some were lost, some refused to move on, and others were determined to communicate with me. I noticed that many of them wanted to relay a message or lesson.

Eventually, I figured out that my house wasn't haunted. I was just being visited by Spirit. Everywhere I went I had an ability to see, hear and feel Spirit all around me.

My ability to connect with God and Spirit and experience these messages and gifts as a child added to the feeling of being different. All I wanted to do was to fit in. One of the important messages I can recall receiving was when I was in eighth grade.

I was home from school babysitting my sister, Sarah. My family had a plumbing business and my dad and grandfather did all of the fieldwork, while my mom and grandmother did the office work.

That night, Mom called home around dinnertime. "Erica, Grandpa's not feeling well and I'm driving him to the hospital in the next town to be checked. Everything will be fine. Finish up your chores if you haven't yet, and watch Sarah until I get home."

As I hung up the phone, I clearly heard a familiar voice telling me that my grandpa was going to die and he was not coming home from the hospital. I knew that voice and had grown a connection with it. I knew that Grandpa was going to have a heart attack. I panicked and as I did, I heard the voice again. It told me to call my uncle, who was my grandpa's oldest child. He lived four hours away in Omaha, Nebraska.

My hands shook as I picked up the telephone and dialed. "Uncle John, it's Erica. Grandpa is on the way to the hospital. He's not going to make it and if you want to say good-bye, you have to drop everything and go now!"

"Slow down now, Erica. How do you know this?"

"God told me and he wants to give you the chance to say goodbye. If you listen to me, you'll be able to see him one more time before he goes to Heaven."

My uncle began to pray and when he finished he said, "Okay, Erica. I believe you. I'm leaving now."

He arrived at the hospital within moments of my grandpa passing away from a heart attack. My parents were shocked and asked him how he knew to come to the hospital when he did.

Uncle John said, "Erica knew what was going to happen. She said God told her."

My uncle thanked me profusely for what I had done.

But I said, "Don't thank me, thank God."

We didn't have cell phones at the time this happened and there was no way during his drive that he could have stopped and checked with my parents. They didn't call my uncle because they didn't know how serious Grandpa's condition was and they didn't want to worry him needlessly. I am so glad I had the courage to share the message with him and he had the opportunity to say good-bye to his father.

As I think back on the experience, I know that if I had doubted who the message was coming from or worried what my uncle might think about me saying such things, I might never have passed along the message, and he would have missed the opportunity that God gave him to say goodbye to his father. I've learned through the years to trust the messages I hear from God and spirit and to do my best to share them with people.

A few years later, I awoke in the middle of the night and sat up. I had left the door to my bedroom open and I could see across the hall into my parent's room. My grandpa, who had passed away, was hunched over my dad as if he had just given him a kiss on the cheek while he slept. He looked at me and I felt very strongly that he had concern for my dad's health and well-being. I knew he was checking on him to see if he was doing okay.

The next morning I shared my experience from the night before. My dad was always the type of person who didn't show much emotion but I noticed a tear slip out as I shared his father's visit with him. I know he was touched knowing his father was still nearby.

When I was young, something else happened and I wouldn't grasp the significance of the event until years later. I was attending a church-sponsored women's assembly in a large banquet room. The participants were all enjoying each other's company and chatting amongst themselves. Their laughter and joy filled the entire room. Then a voice rang out and called for everyone's attention.

As we all took our seats, a small group of women gathered at the front of the room and began to act out a skit of some sort. I don't recall the theme, but I clearly remember watching my good friend's mother. She had the most beautiful smile on her face as she came skipping in for her part in the play. She stopped abruptly, turned and looked at the audience. As I watched her mouth move, I tracked her lips with my eyes, but I couldn't hear what she was saying.

Suddenly, our gazes locked and I watched, frozen, as a series of events unfolded. The woman fell to the floor unconscious. Her human body collapsed around her, yet she was still standing there staring at me at the same time. Even though I was a young girl, at that very moment, I knew that she was fine, like the others who had come to me and communicated with telepathy. She was leaving the vehicle she had used during her Earthly Journey.

Like a butterfly leaves its cocoon and flies away, so did my friend's mother. The butterfly didn't die; it awakened and continued its journey. With telepathy, she told me that she was leaving and that it was time to continue her journey. She promised me that everything would be all right. Then she smiled at me, turned to her left and skipped away just as she had previously entered into the room.

But this time when she moved away from me, I could see that her silhouette was glowing. She was so beautiful and radiant. In her hand was a picnic basket. She shifted and then moved with purpose and power because she was filled with a joy I had never seen before. I watched her scamper to the exit of the fellowship hall. A portal appeared in the air from nowhere and just beyond it was the most beautiful place I had ever seen.

She made a quick exit right into it. I knew where she was going. She was leaving for Heaven. At this point, two things happened. First I thought, *wow, I want to go too!* And the second thing was, I immediately felt an incredible burning sensation in my eyes. I think I had forgotten to blink. I blinked a few times to relieve the burn. It was only for a moment, but when I looked up again, she was gone.

My attention was drawn from that side of the room to the commotion and chaos happening in the fellowship hall. The woman's physical body lay lifeless on the floor as people rushed to try to help her. I knew that their attention wasn't going to make a difference. At that point, it didn't matter what they tried to do; no medical intervention would be able to awaken her into that body again.

I struggled, wondering if I should share what I had seen with my friend. On one hand, I was given an incredible gift. I was so excited for my friend's mother because I knew she didn't really die. On the other hand, I knew that this knowledge would not have the ability to take away the pain of her absence. I continued to try to make sense of all of this when I heard a familiar voice drown out the noise around me. It was God and He reassured me that everything would be okay. She worked for Him now and it was time for her new job in Heaven.

I know in my heart it was important that she left, and my feeling was that somehow, for whatever reason, someone needed her help there too. God told me that she would always be with my friend because there was no separation between here and Heaven.

Feeling terribly conflicted, part of me wanted to share what I had seen, but I didn't want to say the wrong thing to my friend and hurt him in any way. I also didn't want to be thought of as crazy. It was already hard enough at school, and this experience only added to my burden of feeling different. What I didn't know at the time was that this ability was a gift from God and it was just unfolding in my youth.

# DESTINY OR DESIRE

*"For I know the plans I have for you, declares the Lord, plans for welfare and not for evil, to give you a future and a hope."*

Jeremiah 29:11 (ESV)

I continued to hide my unusual abilities from the kids at school because things were already difficult enough. I didn't want to give them any more reasons to make fun of me. In fact, I was thrilled to finally graduate high school and leave the pettiness behind me.

I just knew that the college experience would be different, but I was so disheartened when I encountered more of the same gossip, back stabbing and judgment. I continued to take it out on myself and ended up hospitalized for bulimia. This self-destructive behavior had done such damage to my body. The doctors discovered ulcers in the esophagus and stomach. My family tried to help me, but I didn't want to face my problems and refused to talk about bulimia. Besides bulimia, I also suffered from chronic endometrioses that presented itself with acute symptoms of abdominal pain. This had started in the sixth grade. As I look back, I concluded the eating disorder didn't help, but the endometrioses quickly went from acute to chronic at an early age. I was in and out of emergency rooms with acute attacks of pain.

One of the problems was the constant battle with my weight. This was caused by a hormone imbalance due to my endometriosis, which wasn't properly diagnosed or treated for several years. This continued into college.

Despite health issues, I was excited to major in the field of Television Broadcasting. I wanted to be the next Barbara Walters.

As a child, I spent many Saturday nights watching television with my grandparents. We had a ritual. Grandma would make popcorn and root beer floats and we would sit with Grandpa and watch *Lawrence Welk*, followed by *Archie Bunker's Place* and *The Jefferson's*. I hardly paid attention to the television because I was too busy styling their hair. Unfortunately for Grandpa, I somehow managed to part his hair into small clumps, which were still ample enough to wrap around and secure to Grandma's rollers. I'm quite sure he had at least eight or nine rollers in his hair by the time our beauty session was complete.

Afterward, I would use the hairbrush as a microphone. I'd take turns interviewing them both to get the full story because Grandma taught me the story was so important. They told me everything about their lives, their dreams and any events they were planning to attend and I loved interviewing them. I'm not sure why but I felt I was born to deliver the news.

When the evening's festivities ended, she'd tuck me into my bed in the guestroom and we would engage in small talk for a bit. Then she would direct my gaze to the picture on the wall by the bed, a picture of Jesus walking on a narrow road talking with two people. I reflected on that picture as I imagined Jesus sharing stories about God and His love for us.

My grandma would look at me and say, "Now Erica, one day when you are telling your stories, don't forget why they're so important." I think she meant for me to recall who these stories came from and how they were supposed to empower and help people, just like the stories and teachings Jesus shared.

With that, she'd turn out the light and let me contemplate her words as I fell asleep. Some nights I would lie on my side staring at that picture as the light from the moon found its way into the window, illuminating it just enough for me to view it until I eventually drifted off to sleep.

My grandma passed away several years later when I was pregnant with my first child. I wondered how Grandma knew so much about what I would be doing, but somehow she did. As an adult, I'm able to look back on it now and see how she was instrumental in helping to prepare me for the mission I was to experience in the future. I am reminded how important her words were about sharing my stories with people.

How was my grandma able to know what I'd be doing many years in the future? The only answer I can imagine was she let God use her as a vehicle to do the work, and part of her job and mission was to help guide me.

As a freshman, I worked at the college TV station reporting the news. Bursting with excitement, I was on my way to changing the world and this time, I had a real microphone with real stories from real people. It was awesome! I was finally beginning to implement the skills I'd been practicing since that first interview in my grandparent's living room with the hairbrush. It felt so natural. I just knew this was what I was meant to do, but destiny intervened.

Destiny had a name and it was Derek McKenzie. He was 6"1 with dirty blonde hair, freckles and eyes that would change color from blue to green like a chameleon depending on the clothes he was wearing. He was a senior studying business administration at the same college. He was also president of his fraternity house and saw me reporting the news on the college television station one day. Determined to meet me, he coordinated an introduction by enlisting the help of one of his fraternity brothers. His fraternity brother was dating one of my sorority sisters. We met in May of 1990. Honestly, it was love at first sight. He was just getting ready to graduate and got a great job in Omaha, Nebraska. I was determined to pursue a career in broadcasting and my counselor suggested that colleges on either coast would be a better choice than the one in Nebraska.

But my heart knew the difference between desire and destiny. In my case, the two were leading in opposite directions. I desired nothing more than to be the next Barbara Walters. It was a desire, a *knowing* I had held since childhood, and I was finally on a course to have the opportunity to move one-step closer to my goal.

But Derek was my destiny, and God wouldn't relieve me of that message. Looking back now, I know the poor guy didn't realize what he had signed up for, but God did. Derek was the love of my life and so I chose love. I chose to listen to God.

In choosing my love for Derek, I had to let go of my dream of becoming the next Barbara Walters. Derek was going to stay in Nebraska and I couldn't fathom being away from him, so I made the decision to stay with him and switch majors instead. As I contemplated a new major, I remembered that my grandmother worked as an assistant to the doctor in her town who delivered babies. She loved helping people. That's it, I thought. I love helping people too. I'll become a nurse. This was a job that would allow me to work in the Midwest and study at a college close to Derek.

We were married in June of 1993. It was a milestone for me and I have wonderful memories of the beautiful wedding we shared. I loved my husband so much, but I had a dark secret not even Derek knew.

# MY DARK SECRET

*"For the Lord sees not as man sees: man looks on the outward appearance, but the Lord looks on the heart."*

1 Samuel 16:7 (ESV)

My first job out of college as a nurse was working for a group of dermatologists. I enjoyed the job. While there, I was introduced to two of the most widely prescribed drugs or drug combinations for weight loss and weight control. Fen-Phen is a combination of Fenfluramine (Pondimin) and Phentermine (Adipex), sold separately but prescribed in combination.

At 125 pounds, I decided to try Fen-Phen because I felt I needed to lose ten pounds to reach my perfect weight. I was running four miles a day, binging and purging my food, and just couldn't drop those last few pounds. While on the drug, I experienced changes in my mood and an increase in labored breathing upon resting. That scared me. One of my nurse colleagues had experienced something similar and stopped taking the Fenfluramine (Pondimin). But she continued to take Phentermine (Adipex). She reported that by doing this, her side effects were diminished. At her suggestion, I followed in her footsteps.

As I mentioned, Phentermine is the generic name for Adipex, a class four narcotic. Twelve weeks was the recommended therapeutic amount of time to take Phentermine under a doctor's supervision. As a nurse, I understood the importance of having routine exams and blood work done to ensure that I stayed healthy, but I didn't go get the blood work done. I loved the way the weight fell off me. I rationalized that because I felt fine and the doctor continued prescribing it to me without requiring a blood test or exam, I didn't need it. Only later did I realize that this was a bad decision.

The choice to take the drug was easy. I was exhausted by the mere thought of the work it took to binge and purge multiple times a day. It had consumed me for years. On the drug, I felt free. I was no longer a prisoner to my routine. For the first time in twelve long years, I didn't have to think about throwing up the food I had just ingested. This drug completely took away my appetite and I felt ill if I tried to eat. I had traded the serious addiction of bulimia for one that could be fatal.

In my desperation to "fit in" and reach my ideal weight, I ignored the potential risks from the dangerous and life-threatening side effects of the drug, and then compounded my risk by disregarding the necessary blood tests and doctor supervision.

In the spring of 1996, my husband started a new job in Denver, Colorado and at the same time the FDA released a new approved drug called Dexfenfluramine (Redux). This new drug was required to be labeled for weight loss and long-term weight maintenance, but the FDA cautioned that studies had only lasted one year. Dexfenfluramine sales went through the roof and it was taken by a total of two million Americans.

I was pregnant at the time with my first child, so I was not able to take the drug. However, following the birth of my son that September, I contacted a new doctor in fear that I would not be able to lose the seventy pounds of post-pregnancy weight. My doctor prescribed Redux. I lost seventy pounds in approximately four months. I continued to take the Redux, but only for a short period of time, because it was withdrawn from the market within a year of being approved. In fact, in September of 1997, both the diet drugs Pondimin and Redux were withdrawn from the market. When my doctor was no longer able to prescribe the Redux, I switched back to Phentermine (Adipex).

One of the most serious side effects linked to the drugs was Primary Pulmonary Hypertension or PPH, a serious lung disease where the blood vessels constrict and create abnormally high blood pressure. Unfortunately, PPH is usually a permanent condition and in many instances can lead to death. Other side effects included shortness of breath, chest pain, swelling of extremities, palpitations, and heart valve leakage. Valve damage is generally a silent condition, causing no symptoms to the patient, until the condition becomes severe. In addition to these cardio-pulmonary complications, many individuals also experienced neurotransmitter deficiencies.

People with neurotransmitter deficiencies can suffer changes in brain function, inability to concentrate, learning disorders, depression, anxiety, panic attacks, PMS, menopausal symptoms, obesity, impulsive behavior, fatigue, fibromyalgia, low libido, insomnia, short-term memory loss, headaches, irritability, personality changes, depression and more.

Dieting and eating disorders are the most common cause of self-induced neurotransmitter deficiencies. In addition, long-term use of diet pills can deplete neurotransmitter stores. Diet pills like Phen-fen, and Phentermine use up large amounts of dopamine and serotonin, which can result in a multitude of health issues.

Prolonged emotional or physical stress, abnormal sleep, and inflammatory conditions like endometriosis can all compound the severity of the neurotransmitter deficiencies.

In 1997, several users of Fen-Phen or Redux reported many of these side effects and damage from taking these drugs. As a result, lawsuits and class action suits were filed against the drug manufacturers.

We had built a new home overlooking the mountains and were excited about being parents to our infant son. Our house shared a backyard fence with the neighbor. This neighbor became my beloved best friend. Her name was Jennifer. She was everything I ever desired in a relationship with a girlfriend. She made me laugh, we shared stories, and we were always there for each other. We had no interest in gossip. We were too busy building others up with our optimism.

Both of our husbands were very good at their jobs. They were dedicated and hard-working, and they both put in a lot of hours. They were both climbing the corporate ladder at a fast pace. Jennifer's husband's job required him to travel frequently and in 1997, Derek's job required us to move back to Omaha, Nebraska. I was devastated. We were barely there a year and had just settled into our new home. I was so happy and now I would be separated from my best friend.

During these years, the only period of time I wasn't taking my weight loss drug was during my two pregnancies. I loved my babies and would never do anything to potentially harm them.

In the fall of 1999, we left Nebraska and moved to Kansas City, Kansas, just in time for me to give birth to my second child. Despite running several miles a day into my ninth month, I gained almost seventy pounds with this pregnancy as well. Following the birth, several people mentioned how difficult it would be to drop my post pregnancy weight, especially the second time around. This was the last thing I needed to hear and suddenly I was afraid that I would never lose the weight.

Memories and feelings of the ridicule and bullying I experienced in the past returned with a vengeance. It seemed everyone was concerned with how I looked and I couldn't get away from the pressure to be thin. These messages were everywhere, from the tabloids and magazine covers in the grocery checkout line, on television, and even in the sideways glances from strangers. The pressure of society's expectations of what was an acceptable physical appearance was too much and, once again, I found myself trying to fit in.

More determined than ever, I set out to find a weight loss specialist to help me. After thorough research, I discovered a doctor of bariatrics; a licensed medical professional with a list of credentials. The doctor appeared confident, knowledgeable, attentive, caring and supportive of my needs, so I didn't think twice when I was not required to have follow up medical exams or blood tests. When my doctor suggested I take Fenfluramine, I assumed the FDA had reapproved it for the United States market. After expressing my concerns about my initial reaction and side effects to the drug, I was given assurance that I should be fine. After all, it had been years since I first tried it, so I decided to take the doctor's advice and try the Fenfluramine again.

What I didn't know at the time was that my doctor was under investigation by the FBI. During the time I was a patient, this doctor had moved offices several times. In fact, at one point, I visited a rented storage locker to buy my prescriptions. I remember thinking how odd it was having a doctor visit that was staged out of a storage locker. When I asked for an explanation, the doctor easily brushed it off as a temporary misunderstanding. I sensed something was wrong but because I was addicted to the drugs, I chose to ignore my concerns.

My doctor insisted on cash for my prescriptions. Unbeknownst to me, the diet drugs were a huge moneymaker, and in accordance with the doctor's instructions, when necessary, I drove across state lines to fill my prescriptions at one specific pharmacy. Disconcerting was the fact that the pharmacy continued to fill my prescriptions for nearly three years without question.

In 2001, I began to exhibit several less than desirable symptoms, both physical and mental, so I scheduled an appointment to discuss them with my doctor. During this visit, I was educated on HGH, human growth hormone. This was a daily injection effective for weight loss, among other things. The doctor suggested I was a candidate for the treatment. In addition, according to him, it could possibly help to relieve my symptoms, improve concentration, memory, help me gain lean muscle and maintain fat loss. In fact, my doctor mentioned using it personally.

This sounded like the fountain of youth, so I was definitely interested, but when I found out the monthly cost of the HGH, I knew there was no way I could afford it. Therefore, I was switched to Phentermine and added the medications Bontril, Modulator and Armour Thyroid to my regimen.

I was always required to pay out of pocket using cash for my doctor visits and prescriptions. In spite of all these new prescriptions, never once did I get examined or have blood work. If I didn't go to the doctor visit, I wouldn't get the prescriptions, which meant I wouldn't get the drugs. The cost of the visits and the drugs were well over three hundred dollars a month. This was not only a dirty little secret, but an expensive one as well.

I had tried practically every new diet on the market. Let's see, there was the Adkins diet, Weightwatchers, the Watermelon diet, even the cabbage soup diet, to name a few. But the Fenfluramine and Phentermine worked the best. In fact, in college, unbeknownst to my parents, I had cut my cafeteria card up, limiting myself to twenty dollars a month to spend on food, ensuring I couldn't eat even if I wanted to. It's embarrassing to admit but I even had liposuction and took diuretics and enemas to lose weight.

My heart knew this wasn't what God wanted me to do. He wanted me to love and accept myself as He did, but I just couldn't stop. I desperately wanted to fit in and I thought that being skinny would help me do it.

By taking the diet drug, I rationalized I could break my bulimia habit. I'd been bulimic for twelve long years and had grown extremely weary of having to binge and purge everything that was consumed. My knuckles were scarred and my throat and stomach lining felt raw and burned. The pain was intense. I also had broken blood vessels called Petechiae on my face, in my eyes, and on my neck. I would not begin to understand the amount of damage the bulimia had caused my neurotransmitters until several years later.

Derek and I were inseparable and it was becoming more challenging to hide my bulimia from him. The Phentermine was the perfect solution.

Despite all this, it was still difficult to find friends who didn't gossip and criticize. I found myself thinking, if they gossiped in front of me about other people, what were they saying about me behind my back? This really bothered me. I wanted to be liked. I thought the move to Kansas would be a fresh start, but the majority of women I encountered seemed to be the same kind of women I'd met in high school and college who gossiped and judged.

When Derek and I moved from Omaha to Kansas City, I thought things would be different. Call me optimistic, unrealistic, even crazy, but I've always had a positive way of looking at things. I can't help it, I guess I get that from my mom. I truly thought that once I was married and had kids, the mothers with whom I would associate would be the loving, kind and positive people I had always hoped to meet and call my friends. I thought how wonderful it would be to finally have a group of real friends with whom our kids could grow up and make memories together.

As a stay-at-home mom, I looked forward to being able to have some adult conversation with other parents. We were finally settled into our new home. It was the first day of kindergarten for my oldest child, Keenan.

With my trusty cup of coffee in hand, we stood together, waiting in anticipation for the bus. Parents with children began to congregate and conversations swirled in the air with the usual, "Good morning!" or "How are you this beautiful morning?" or "I am so and so, it's a pleasure to meet you. Welcome to the neighborhood." I smiled and breathed a sigh of relief. Everything appeared to be normal. And then it happened.

The conversation changed to gossip. Shocked by how quickly the pleasantries were replaced with cutting comments about people and other children, I realized that these negative conversations were all within earshot of our young kids. I now understood why there were mean children in this world. It never occurred to me that it was quite possible this behavior started with the parents.

I was so disillusioned, I completely withdrew and spent the majority of my time trying to be the best mother and wife I could be. I avoided the parent meetings, block parties, and mommy groups because I just couldn't take all the negativity. I always imagined a world where people would just stop gossiping and start appreciating each other despite their differences. This would be an ideal way to empower each other.

When I tried to share these thoughts and feelings, the familiar response was always the same, "Erica, you're crazy to think that you are capable of changing things. You're only one person and it's always going to be like this. It was true, I was only one person but as for the rest of it? Something inside me refused accept that changing the world was not possible. I felt certain it didn't have to be this way. No matter how hard I tried, I couldn't let go of that thought. I felt such conviction and determination to put action to the knowing that I had, but it was going to take much more than a girl from Kansas to make that happen.

I didn't know how to get started; yet I couldn't let that feeling go. I cared about more than just my little world, in my little suburb, on my little cul-de-sac. I cared about the big picture and about really making a difference. I missed my best friend, Jennifer, more than ever. She was living proof that other women existed, that weren't related to me, who saw the world like I did.

In the meantime, I continued with the diet drugs for nearly nine years. There were two major side effects of this drug for me. I barely ate or slept. And they also gave me an abundance of energy. Derek's job required that he rise very early, so by the time evening rolled around he was exhausted. He would get in bed and I followed. The moment he was fast asleep, I would get out of bed, get dressed and get to work on whatever project I was involved in at the time.

At one point, I was outside landscaping our house in the middle of the night. I positioned floodlights beside me, bringing a small amount of light to aid in digging irrigation ditches in our front yard. Even the neighbor noticed and questioned me but it did little to dissuade me from continuing to take the drug.

The Phentermine drove me relentlessly. I just couldn't stop. Many nights I would scare Derek when I sprung out of bed and jumped up and down. It felt as if my heart was barely pumping. I couldn't catch my breath. The jumping seemed to circulate the blood and force air into my lungs. Were my lungs forgetting how to do their job? I wasn't overweight, but my heart felt like it was working overtime. I didn't realize that the diet pills were slowly killing me.

I understand now how important it is to be under a doctor's supervision while on medication, but back then, I was too concerned about my weight and rationalized the symptoms. After all, close to nine years had passed, and I was still taking the diet pills my doctor happily continued to prescribe for me. I went to see the doctor every month with my cash in hand. I never missed an appointment for the prescription and the doctor never refused to prescribe it.

My doctor was a qualified expert practicing bariatrics, the field of medicine concerned with weight loss. I told myself if I was allowed to take this medication, then it had to be okay. After all, the doctor was the expert. There was a brief moment when I considered that the doctor could be wrong, but I quickly dismissed that idea because I didn't think I could live without the drug. And I certainly didn't want the alternative—bulimia. I didn't even care that the doctor had moved office locations multiple times and that my current appointments brought me to an old storage unit for my prescription.

Over the years, the drug had taken a major toll on my body. During that time, I had manic episodes of highs and lows and exhibited behavior that resembled bipolar disorder. Anyone with medical knowledge knows it is highly unlikely that I was developing bipolar disorder in my thirties with no family history and no prior symptoms of mental illness.

Through it all, my husband was by my side. I couldn't have survived all these years without his help. Out of concern for my health, Derek pulled me aside one day and expressed his great concern, "I don't know what's wrong with you, but you can't keep going like this. It's affecting me and the children."

I argued with him to explain my behavior and that I would try to be better. I knew he was reaching out and wanted to help me and I desperately wanted to tell him my dirty little secret, but I couldn't. I had a choice to come clean at that moment, yet I chose the drugs over my family and my relationship with my husband.

"Erica, listen to me," he ordered. "I want you to go away with Jennifer for a long weekend and just relax." Jennifer still resided in Denver, Colorado so we were only able to see each other once a year. I always looked forward to our weekend together. It was my opportunity to be myself, and included hours of laughter and girl talk, free from female judgment

But Derek was right. I was exhausted and it was affecting my ability to care for our two young children. My children were my life. I loved them more than anything. I made plans to fly to Las Vegas to meet Jennifer

As I glanced up at my husband and his dark furrowed brow, I could see the frustration and concern in his eyes. He so desperately wanted to help me. I closed my eyes, ashamed of the worry I had caused him. A few days later, we stood in the kitchen and I hugged my family good- bye. It was always difficult to leave them, especially my babies. I would miss them terribly. Derek's serious green eyes caught and held my attention. His stare matched his tone. "Rest," he ordered.

I nodded, fully intending to do so. "I love you," I said as I grabbed my briefcase and purse and headed for the door.

In a few short days, I would be dead.

# ANGEL ON THE AIRCRAFT

*"When you call to me, I will answer you. I will be with you
when you are in trouble. I will save you and honor you."*

Psalm 91:15 (God's Word)

Time was running out. My trip to Las Vegas with my best
friend was supposed to have been a relaxing long
weekend of rest and rejuvenation. Instead of lying by
the pool or spending time at the spa, we filled our days with
shopping and enjoyed the nightlife and excitement. We barely
stopped to eat or sleep, which frankly, I rarely did anyway.

Jennifer was a wonderful friend, however, the reality was
Jennifer lived far away and I missed her. At the time, we both
had young children at home and we could only get together
once a year. We would pick a place and fly to that destination
to meet. I could just be myself around Jennifer, so when we got
together we'd make each hour count.

When Jennifer first saw me in Las Vegas, she was
concerned. She knew me so well that she could tell
something was very wrong. I treated her like Derek when she
tried to ask me about my health. I lied. I promised that I
was fine, just worn out from the daily activities of motherhood
and the household projects I'd taken on.

The truth was, my Phentermine use had taken a dangerous
toll on my body, I barely ate or slept. My body didn't receive

the nutrients it needed, nor did I rest enough to allow it to rebuild each night. Little did I know the drug use had also affected my heart and lungs.

Each night when it was time to retire to our beds, we'd reflect upon the fun we had that day. I'd hide my exhaustion up until the moment I knew she had drifted off to sleep. When I tried to relax and drift off to sleep myself, I could feel my lungs forgetting to do the job they had done since birth. I couldn't allow myself to fall asleep, but I needed to desperately. As I exhaled, my lungs weren't automatically refilling themselves with air. It was as if they had forgotten how to inflate. It seemed that the part of my brain that normally sent the signal to my lungs to fill with air had forgotten how to send that message.

I couldn't risk falling asleep. Part of me was terrified my lungs would forget to work and the other part was concerned about alarming Jennifer and exposing my secret by leaping out of bed and jumping up and down to force air into my lungs.

So I chose to lie in bed each night and talk to God while my friend slept. *God, I know I can't continue taking these drugs. I can't continue to ignore what they're doing to me. My symptoms are getting worse and I'm really scared because I feel like the drugs are going to kill me if something doesn't change. I need a different plan. I know I have to listen to you; I just need a little more time.*

I found myself bargaining with God to help get me through the weekend and promised that when I returned to Kansas City I would figure things out.

Jennifer and I said our goodbyes at the airport and boarded our respective planes. I took the last flight home for the evening to Kansas City. My heart was sad to leave my best friend. I had enjoyed her company so much, but I was beyond exhaustion.

With little rest or food, my weary body began to shut down. It was harder to draw each breath and a wave of dizziness hit me as I moved down the aisle of the plane. Once seated on the aisle, I stowed my laptop beneath the seat in front of me, but I had to shove the case with my foot to get it to fit. Now it was wedged beneath the seat and the floor. Our taxi to the runway took longer than normal and people began to pull out projects to work on. The young girl seated by the window in my row pulled out her book to read. I couldn't sleep so I tried to reach for my laptop and some paper stowed inside, but concluded it was indeed stuck. I was too weary to pry it free, and instead leaned back and closed my eyes.

The airplane's takeoff was rather abrupt and pressed my already worn body deeply into the seat. It felt as though the plane made an unusually steep ascent upwards. We reached altitude a few minutes later along with extreme turbulence and instinctively, I cinched my seatbelt tighter across my lap. Just as I did, my seatbelt dug into my hips as the plane dipped and shuddered in a violent retort on its high-speed route toward Kansas City.

Rain pounded the plane as we flew into the direct path of a thunderstorm. Lightning flashed outside and water raced in rivulets across the window. Above me, the overhead bins rattled, shifting their contents and testing the latches on the doors. It sounded as if the plane was being ripped apart around us. I gripped the armrests of my seat until my knuckles turned white. The lights flickered in the cabin. The fierce turbulence was more than I could handle and I squeezed my eyes shut against the inevitable. Trembling, tears streamed down my cheeks. I was terrified and quite certain that we were going to crash.

All I could think about were my babies. I couldn't bear to leave them motherless and my heart broke at the thought. Would I ever see them again, hold them close and tell them how much I loved them? Fear consumed me. I felt a powerful surge of adrenaline. I had to get out of there, to safety, to my babies, but there was nowhere to run. I had no one to turn to except God, so I tilted my face toward Heaven and cried out, *"God, help me!"*

The world shifted into slow motion and I noticed the couple on my right as they embraced each other. I read his lips. "She's crying," he said to his pregnant wife. I can't think of any words that describe the magnitude of what it feels like when you know you're going to die.

I desperately wanted to see my children again, I pleaded silently, *God save me. Let me live and I promise I will dedicate my life to working for you.* Suddenly, I could no longer contain my pleading to God and I prayed aloud with the only words I knew that might comfort me. "Our Father, who art in Heaven, hallowed be thy name. Thy kingdom come, Thy will be done…"

A flight attendant appeared in the aisle. Her gaze captured and held mine. "…on earth as it is in Heaven," I continued. Mesmerized by her sheer beauty, her radiance and calm demeanor, I could focus on nothing but her as she moved in my direction with purpose, unfazed by the turbulence. She was immaculately dressed in a navy blue skirt and crisp white blouse. Her golden blonde hair fell in waves across her shoulders and over a scarf tied neatly at her neck.

"…Give us this day our daily bread." *Dear God, she's coming towards me!* I thought as she slipped into the aisle seat beside me and buckled up. The plane lurched and dropped several feet, sending us forcefully upward against our seat belts. Just as I thought *this is it, this is the end*, peace flooded my entire body.

I felt compelled to look at her and when I did, she said, *"Be quiet and listen. You are going to write a letter to God and ask him to save you because you need help."*

As I glanced down at the pen and paper in my hand, I wondered how they got there. It was the paper from my briefcase, yet the case was still stuck beneath the seat in front of me.

Our eyes met once more and the woman gently nodded in the direction of the paper. There was something so familiar about her, peaceful and serene. I acknowledged her nod, putting pen to paper and began to write. For some reason the turbulence didn't seem to hamper me.

### Dear God and My Children,

I love you all more than anything, more than life here on earth, but God, I'm not ready to give that up yet. I can't. I won't accept it. I will not allow myself to think of a moment in life where my children wouldn't be with me, to touch them, to smell them, to hold them. Those very gifts are all that I care to hold on to.

God, I love existing because of them and living because I have a purpose. My work isn't done here. I can't do this, God. I am terrified! Save me God, and let me live another day, a day that will give me the chance to hold those amazing children that you gave me just one more time! That's all I am asking from you. And God, if you do this one thing for me, I promise, I will work for you for the rest of my life. Give me that contract right now. Let me sign it because I'm ready. There is no doubt in my mind that there is nothing more powerful than you, so make this happen. Please, God! I am here God, and I am ready! Are you listening, God?

I love you all,
Love, Erica

As I poured my heart and soul into the letter, I hoped that someone might recover it and give it to my children if we crashed. Vivid memories of my children filled my thoughts with each word I wrote, and by the time I finished writing the letter an overwhelming sense of peace flooded my body.

The turbulence stopped and the plane returned to a normal, smooth flight. I looked up and knew in my heart that the plane would land safely because God had heard my prayers and rescued me. It seems strange to think of now, but I had the eerie feeling that by crying out to God to save me, I had also saved the plane and those on board.

The flight attendant sat patiently with me as I wrote my letter to God, and when I'd finished we began to talk. There was something so familiar about her, the way she spoke with kindness and compassion in her voice. It felt as if I had always known her. I asked about her life and shared stories about mine. Our conversation was effortless, yet so deeply meaningful to me. The hours passed quickly. Excluding family, I had never had such a sense of ease and companionship with another woman aside from Jennifer. It was the kind of relationship I'd always hoped to find in high school and college.

Sitting there with this compassionate flight attendant and feeling accepted and liked for just being me was all I had ever wanted. My entire life had been spent searching for someone with whom I had so much in common.

Deep down I was touched that this stranger, a woman, would take the time to sit with me the entire flight, and keep me calm. Filled with gratitude for her sincere care and compassion, I deeply appreciated the kindness she had shown me.

The crackle of the loud speaker interrupted our conversation. "Ladies and gentleman we'll be landing in Kansas

City in a few minutes. Flight attendants, please prepare the cabin for landing."

She smiled at me one last time, rose and walked to the front of the plane, disappearing from my sight as she entered the First Class cabin. I didn't want her to go and an unexpected emptiness filled my heart at her absence. I needed to thank her for her kindness in helping me.

Once we landed and arrived at the gate, I waited for everyone to deplane. I wanted to pull the kind flight attendant aside and really express my gratitude for what she had done. I wrestled with and freed my briefcase, and headed to the exit.

As I reached the front of the cabin, I addressed the nearest flight attendant, "Excuse me. I'm looking for the stewardess with the long blonde hair...really nice woman."

She looked at her co-worker next to her, a middle- aged woman with dark hair. "I'm sorry ma'am. I don't know who you are referring to."

I glanced at the paper and pen still in my hand. "She gave me this to write a letter and I wanted to thank her."

"I'm sorry, ma'am. There isn't a blond flight attendant on this plane."

Bewildered by her answer, I made my way off the plane. The high I had felt talking with the blond flight attendant vanished, replaced by a weariness that went deep into my bones. Suddenly, I barely had the strength to retrieve my luggage and head to the parking lot for the long drive home.

It was 11 p.m. I wasn't physically up for the forty-minute drive, but I had no other option. Rain hammered the windshield and made it difficult to see. This only added to the claustrophobic feeling I had. I felt as if I was suffocating and fought for each breath against the waves of dizziness that accompanied them. As a nurse, I knew my extreme fatigue, heart palpitations, dizziness and shortness of breath were not a good sign.

*I needed help.*

I reached out to the only person I knew who could help me. "God, please help me. I work for you now. I want to do whatever you are calling me to do. But first I need you to help heal me because something is really wrong."

The next thing I recall, I was sitting in my driveway. I honestly don't know how I got there. I can only remember parts of my conversation with Him and very little of the drive home.

Gripping the steering wheel, I stared through the windshield at the house. "Oh God, please give me strength to face my husband. He is going to be so upset seeing me in this condition. I let him down when I told him I would rest and take care of myself and then I didn't."

With what energy I could muster, I dragged myself from the car with my luggage behind me. Derek met me at the door. I didn't want to scare him but I could tell by his expression that I had. I was anything but rested. Waves of guilt and exhaustion washed over me. I could no longer hold myself together and burst into tears.

"Erica, get hold of yourself or you'll wake the kids," he commanded in a loud whisper. He picked me up and carried me to the couch in the basement. "In the morning, I won't tell the kids you're home so you can have all day to rest."

He sat with me until he fell asleep. I wanted so desperately to sleep, but I was physically unable to do so. Each time I tried to lie down my heart rate slowed so much I thought it might stop altogether. Instantly, without thought, I would launch myself into a standing position, then jump up and down several times forcing air into my lungs as my heart began to pump harder. It was a pattern I had developed over nearly nine years from my drug use, but now even that wasn't working.

*I was dying and I didn't even know it.*

# THE FAITH CHOICE

*"Ask, and it shall be given you; Seek, and you shall find;*

*Knock and the door shall be opened to you."*

Matthew 7:7 (ESV)

I don't know how much time passed, or how long I stayed in the basement away from my children, but Derek finally took charge of the situation. "I want you to check into the hotel just up the street and go to bed. The kids can't see you like this. And *this* time I want you to sleep."

It was not a suggestion. It was an order. I'm such a hands-on-mom, I knew there was no way of getting any rest in the house with my two little children upstairs and Daddy watching them. Kids have Mommy Radar and I knew they would eventually find me. Derek was right. A hotel was the best option. I so desperately wanted to tell him that there was something physically wrong with my body but I didn't. I was so ashamed I had let it get this far.

I know now that Derek was very concerned because I hadn't followed his advice to rest on my trip to Las Vegas. He could see that I was getting worse even though I didn't see it myself. He was so concerned that he thought a night in a hotel would allow me to get the rest I needed.

I should've gone to the hospital, not a hotel.

Still wearing the same clothes I'd flown home in, and too weary to consider changing them, I wondered how I'd be able to drive myself to the hotel up the street. Feeling lightheaded, I got in the car and headed down the driveway anyway. I asked God to please protect me while I was driving so that I wouldn't crash and hurt anyone.

Within minutes, I was standing at the front desk of the Holiday Inn waiting to check in. As I leaned against the counter to keep myself from collapsing, the clerk looked at me and said, "I'm sorry miss, there is no room at the Inn." Tears spilled down my cheeks. His face softened and he quickly mentioned a few more hotels up the road, so I thanked him and left.

I don't know why I didn't just drive myself to the nearest emergency room. In fact, I had just driven right past it on the way to the next hotel. Ahead was a small strip of hotels but the decision to choose one seemed overwhelming.

Out of nowhere, a large orange construction sign appeared to my right. The sign read, "Go this way" with an arrow pointing to a small hotel at the end of the road. I couldn't recall having seen a construction sign that read, "Go this way" before and thought it quite odd. I hesitated and immediately heard God's voice say, *"Go, Erica."*

So I did and pulled into the parking lot of the small hotel. Even in my condition, I noticed that each car in the lot had a different out-of-state license plate; no two were the same. "How peculiar," I thought. I turned off the ignition and sat there a moment trying to gather the strength it would take to walk inside the hotel.

As a nurse, I noticed my labored breathing and a wave of fear shot through me. I was truly afraid my lungs could no longer hold enough air to sustain me. Another wave of dizziness hit and I closed my eyes for a moment. Through sheer will power, I dragged myself from my car to register.

This hotel was different from any I had stayed at in the past. It had an open courtyard and you entered through the front of the hotel, got your key, and then proceeded to go through the lobby into the open courtyard.

As the clerk checked me in, I noticed a newspaper lying on the counter. The headlines read something about a terrorist. It had been a year since 9/11 and everyone was still on edge. I was so distracted by the article, I didn't hear the clerk's directions to my room.

"May I have this paper?" I asked.

"Of course," he answered.

Just as I made my way outside to the courtyard, a huge wave of exhaustion hit me and stars swirled in front of my eyes. I desperately needed to lie down, but I didn't have the strength to go back to the office to ask for my room number. In sheer desperation, I climbed the first set of stairs, praying that it led to my room. I slid my card key in the door. It blinked red.

If I'd had the energy to scream in frustration, I would have. Instead I started to cry. *Dear God, please help me.* The door to the room that wasn't mine opened abruptly and a man stepped out carrying a small brown paper bag. His warm olive skin and dark brown hair framed the bluest eyes I'd ever seen. I was so mesmerized that I couldn't look away. He looked like Jesus. He didn't say a word as I continued to cry and attempted to apologize for bothering him.

He extended his hand and I automatically gave him my key card. There was no room number printed on it. He walked past me and down a few stairs, stopped and turned.

"Come." He motioned with his hand. I had taught my children never to go with strangers, yet here I was following

61

one. God's voice said, *"Be quiet and listen."*

I followed the stranger as if in a trance, yet he wasn't a stranger. My heart knew him. He was the man in my grandma's picture on the wall in the guest bedroom I had admired all those years before. I would have followed him anywhere.

In his presence, I felt completely well and an incredible sensation of oneness came over me. There was an instant life-sustaining connection to this *stranger*, similar yet more powerful than the one I had felt with the blond flight attendant on the plane. I followed Jesus to the opposite side of the courtyard and up another set of stairs. Without hesitation, He slid the card into the key slot and swung the door open.

"Come." He motioned again. It was a single word and yet that word spoke to my heart in volumes. I was so grateful for his help that I invited him inside. He came in and closed the door behind him.

Again, I remembered how often I had warned my children to be careful of strangers and here I had invited a total stranger into my room. I was in no condition to protect myself should something happen. I had made a choice solely based on faith in God that this man would not harm me because I believed that this man was His son.

Our eyes met and when they did, there was no hesitation. I *knew* who he was. I didn't want him to leave. Time stood still as we looked at each other. I asked for his contact information so I could thank him again later but with a heavy accent he said, "Take rest." Then he gently brushed by me and walked out the door. With his absence, my exhaustion returned.

My body was desperate for rest, but I realized I couldn't sit or lie down because I was not able to catch my breath. My mind raced for an alternative. Maybe a bath and the warm steam might help me. After starting the bathwater, I returned to the kitchen area, slipped off my shoes and set my diamond ring near my purse and the newspaper on the counter. The room started to spin and I gripped the counter to steady myself.

In the distance, I could hear the bathwater running. I imagined getting in the tub and closing my eyes, slipping beneath the hot water and letting go, relaxing for the first time in weeks. But for some reason, I happened to glance at the newspaper and saw the word *terrorist*. September 11th flashed through my mind, followed by a vision of the out-of-state license plates in the parking lot. My heart began to pound through my chest as I thought of the Middle Eastern man who had helped me to my room and had carried a brown paper bag in his hand. Logic set in and with it my ego. How could I be so naïve as to think that God loved me so much that he would send his son in person to help me? Who did I think I was? And why would Jesus be carrying a paper bag? I assumed it was his lunch, but instantly concluded it was a bomb!

And although he told me to take rest, he did it not to help save my life but to ensure that I would be in the hotel so that he could take my life when the bomb went off. I suddenly thought, *this man isn't Jesus, God's son or even an angel; he's a terrorist!* I was going to die right there! I knew I had to run to safety, but I didn't have the strength to make my legs move. "God help me!" I cried. What I didn't understand until much later was that God was guiding me in this seemingly irrational thought.

The voice said of God was suddenly clear: *"Erica, be quiet and listen. I will save you. Leave everything behind and follow me."*

I glanced at my purse and diamond ring on the counter and then at the keys to my new BMW car. Instantly, God answered my thoughts.

*"Those are things of this world. You cannot take those where you are going. Those who enter my kingdom can only bring themselves. Your worldly possessions have no value in Heaven."* The bathwater was still running. It would overflow. I knew if I paused to go shut off the water or grab my keys or shoes or even the ring, I would not be saved. I had the choice to listen to my human self, my ego, or listen to God—a voice that had never led me astray. Over the years, I'd stifled that voice. I had chosen ego. Now, in this moment, I would choose again. I had faith in His voice; the voice I'd always known and I wanted to live so I chose God.

A rush of adrenaline forced me out the door and across the courtyard to the exit. I ran as far and as fast as I could away from the hotel. I left my possessions behind. I raced through the parking lot, past my new car and across the freshly paved parking lot next door. Ignoring the pain and the fresh tar on my bare feet, I ran past three construction workers on a smoke break.

"Hey lady, are you okay?" one of them shouted.

I stopped for a brief moment, long enough to catch my breath, gathering enough energy to shout back at them, "There's a bomb about to go off in that hotel! Leave everything behind and follow me. You will be okay, but we have to go; now!"

They looked at me and then at each other. An uncomfortable pause with silence was followed by their howls of laughter. My heart sank. I heard God's voice again.

*"Go now!"* God commanded. *"It is free will."*

I knew what that meant. I couldn't save them. Only they could make the choice to save themselves. My heart ached for them even though they were strangers, but I knew I had to listen and obey the voice of God. After all, I'd heard this voice

64

since childhood. There wasn't much time! I ran because my life depended upon it. I ran because God told me to run.

I no longer felt the pain in my feet, the weakness in my limbs or the struggle for breath. I just ran. Ahead was a busy intersection with a four lane road. There was no time to stop, so I said a prayer as I dashed into traffic, dodging the cars and blaring horns. I had almost reached the other side when I darted in front of a car in the last lane. The driver screeched to a stop, inches from hitting me. I froze, stunned by the narrow escape.

The man jumped from his car, terrified he'd hit me and shouted, "Dios mio! Are you okay?!" The Hispanic man asked, "You need help?"

My heart pounded in my chest. With every beat it felt like it was a like the ticking of a time bomb just waiting to go off. Yes! I needed help but I also knew with every fiber of my human self not to get into this man's car. After all, he was a stranger. As soon as that thought registered in my mind, I heard God's voice again.

*"Get in now."*

My mind screamed danger as I was overcome with more fear than imaginable so I pleaded for God to give me a sign that it would be safe for me to get in his car. As I moved towards the passenger side of the old car that had been stripped of paint, there, through the window on the frayed seat lay the Holy Bible.

It was all I needed to see and know that God was indeed telling me to get in this stranger's car. He'd answered my prayers with a sign. So I chose to listen to God, once again, and not the fear-driven ego of my human self. I got in the car and the stranger drove off.

"Un momento, por favor. I can take you anywhere you

need to go." He pointed at the hotel I had just left. "My paycheck."

"We don't have time for that!" I blurted out. "I need to get as far away from that hotel as possible. My life depends on it!" I didn't realize at the time that I was the bomb that was going to explode.

"No, Senorita, necesito mi cheque de pago. My paycheck!"

The next words I said surprised even me. I was downloaded with a message, but before I could attempt to make sense of it, the words just flew from my mouth. "Rodolfo! Be quiet and listen to me right now because these words are God's words, not mine. God knows you are a Christian man; he sees your heart and he has heard all of your prayers. He wants to answer them. God knows you are working hard in America to help make money for your family in Mexico, one of which is suffering with cancer."

Rodolfo's eyes widened and he recoiled, stunned by what I had just said. We both knew there was no way I could have known his name or anything about his family. The poor man swerved to the side of the road and stopped the car. Trembling, he stared at me as if he'd seen a ghost or an angel. Tears spilled from his eyes.

"We can't stay here. We have to go, now!" I ordered. "There is a man in that hotel with a bomb and he's going to blow up the hotel."

I heard God speak to me again. It was a message for Rodolfo.

"Rodolfo!" God says, "If you truly have faith, help her now. If you help her, I will bless you and your family beyond belief."

Still crying, Rodolfo stared at me, bewildered for a moment, unsure what to do next. Then he grabbed his old cell phone and dialed. After a brief conversation in bits of English and Spanish, Rodolfo hung up, pulled into traffic, and made a U-turn. He headed up the hill toward his church, exactly the direction I had been led to run.

Within minutes, he pulled into the parking lot of Abundant Life Church, where a man was waiting to assist him. I found out later the man's name was Pastor Dan Wakefield. He opened my door, but I didn't have the strength to stand up. The pastor commanded me to get up and the two men, one on each side of me, grabbed under my arms and assisted me inside the church to his office. The pastor had already dialed 911.

Unbeknownst to me, the pastor had been scheduled to attend a lecture at the University of Kansas that day, which had been postponed at the last minute. He had unexpectedly stopped by the church to pick up some paperwork on his way home. As he walked to his office, the main line for the church phone rang. Ordinarily he didn't answer that line, but something nudged him to answer it. It was Rodolfo, asking what he could do to assist me.

They helped me to a chair in the pastor's office opposite his desk. Rodolfo took the other chair and started to cry again, shaken, as the pastor sat down. Rodolfo was talking fast through a mixture of accent and English as he desperately tried to relate what happened. He kept looking at me and said, "God is with her."

The pastor looked to me and asked, "Child, who are you?"

I couldn't answer. I couldn't even remember my name.

"Are you married? Do you have a family?"

I tried to draw a breath, but couldn't. I commanded my lungs to open and fill with air, but they wouldn't and then my heart began to beat, pulsating in tandem with a silent countdown to the detonation of the bomb. In an instant, I had that realization – I was the bomb! Desperate to stop it, I frantically leapt out of my chair and jumped up and down, but this time it didn't work.

In the distance, I could hear the paramedics coming down the hall. They might as well have been miles away because in that moment I knew it was too late. They could not save me.

I wanted to scream, *help me!* But I had no breath to create the words. I was terrified. I was suffocating.

I knew at that very moment, I was going to die.

The pastor was a strong man of substantial size. He sprung from his chair and pounded his fist on the desk. "Speak to me now because I can see it in your eyes. I know where you are going." His voice was fading. "Child! Do you believe in God?!"

With the last ounce of energy I had in my body I cried out, *"I believe in God!"* As I said those words, the bomb exploded, my soul separated from my physical body and I watched from above as my body collapsed to the floor below me.

# THERE'S NO PLACE LIKE HOME

"I once was lost, but now I'm found; was blind, but now I see."

John Newton

As I took my last breath, the most remarkable thing happened. It was instantly replaced with unconditional love. It filled me beyond measure and for the first time in my life, I could really breathe!

There was no pain as I drifted away from my earthly body. At first, I didn't want to go. Suddenly, an angel appeared just above me and to my right. This angelic presence reassured me that everything would be okay.

I looked back at Rodolfo trembling in the corner and I knew he had listened to God. "Can he go too?" I asked the angel.

The angel replied, "It is not yet his time."

As I watched from the ceiling, the paramedics administered an IV and placed an oxygen mask on my face to sustain my body. Then they placed my lifeless body on a stretcher and wheeled it to the ambulance. But I knew it was too late. I was gone from my earthly vehicle and I didn't even care.

One moment, I was hovering near the ceiling with an angel; the next moment, I was pulled with incredible force into a tunnel by what felt proportionate to an enormous hook, similar to the kind they hang a carcass on in a meat locker. This force was substantial enough to separate my soul, which I now distinguish as my true self, from my physical body. It felt as if the hook had penetrated my chest. I know that sounds horribly painful imagining it happening to our human body or shell, but in my new state pain was nonexistent. Rather, I sensed the physical mass which had once contained me was now instantly removed and replaced with access to an exhilarating consciousness.

At first, there was only darkness.

When the darkness appeared to have reached its deepest depths, the tunnel filled with the most brilliant and exceedingly powerful light. Along with this powerful light was the most overwhelming and intoxicating sense of love. The acceleration with which I traveled through the tunnel was supersonic but effortless. I felt light years could not measure it. The pull of the hook was immensely powerful, yet extraordinary. I went up and up, and I knew I was going to Heaven.

It seemed as if I rose infinitely past the stars and farther into the all-encompassing light until I had finally reached the end of the tunnel. Once there the most all-encompassing feeling of love overwhelmed me. My human words cannot accurately describe the enormity of the feeling that filled each cell in my body with more love than imaginable.

This love was so tangible I could touch it. While I could not see a physical image, I distinguished this brilliant Presence as the voice I had heard all my life. It was the voice that told me to run, it was the voice that knew Rodolfo's name, it was the voice that asked me to warn my uncle that his father was dying, and it was the voice that said it loved my left hand.

It was God.

This Presence was so powerful and intense that even with my spiritual eyes, I could not look directly upon it. Questions flooded my mind at light speed. God read my thoughts and answered them simultaneously. It was like speed-reading. This communication was so advanced there was nothing on earth like it.

He brought me close to Him like a parent about to tell a child a story. We stood together with our backs towards Heaven and looked out at the stars. Light radiated all around me.

I was aware that Heaven was right behind me. The most powerful love emanated from this place. There are no human words to describe the degree of this sensation. I knew I was finally home. I never wanted to be separated from that feeling and from God again.

God and I began to communicate. Telepathically He said, *"Look."* I glanced up, and watched the stars separate, creating a lining that revealed a movie screen. In my left ear, I could hear the whirring sound of an old projector as I watched the black and white countdown on the movie screen—three, two and one. The title of the movie appeared on the screen—*The Life Review of Erica McKenzie.*

The movie began and I recognized the tiny baby on the screen. That was me! We proceeded to watch the events in my life from the day I was born until the day I died. I distinctly remember knowing that these were the milestone events in my life. These were the memories that humans focused on, the ones they valued and used as a measure of success.

There were milestones like losing my first tooth, my birthdays and athletic awards, learning to drive a car, graduating from college with my nursing degree, getting married, buying a home, and becoming a mother. Every single memory of every single event that had occurred in my lifetime, regardless of the significance, was shown to me.

Overwhelmed by a true feeling of self-fulfillment and delight, I felt so much joy about all the things I was able to experience while on earth. When I wondered why a specific event had happened, God gave an explanation. I learned that things really do happen for a reason, because it is His plan for us, a plan we choose to participate in before we come to earth. I relived each and every one of the memories as they came on screen and then something remarkable happened. God began to fill me with His unconditional love.

I cried out, "God, I can feel you wrap your arms around me! I feel you holding me." As my life review came to an end, I realized I was not shown anything negative. Until that very moment, I felt I had lived a lifetime in Heaven. Basking in my wonderful memories, God turned to me and handed me a pair of eyeglasses.

I had never worn eyeglasses as I always had perfect vision. These glasses were not your normal pair. They were as big as a small vehicle and I had no idea how I was going to put them on. It seemed impossible. As they came towards me, it was then I understood that with God all things are possible. I found my hands automatically reaching out and drawing them near. By the time they rested upon my face, they fit perfectly, as though they were custom made for me.

God said, *"Now look."*

The stars parted and I heard the sound of the old projector begin again. God and I watched the countdown on the screen—three, two, one. Once again, it started with my birth.

For the first time in my life, I could see! I was stunned. This time I did not see the things that I had seen before. This time I saw every word, thought and action deemed unimportant, insignificant to man. Yet, I now understood the things in life that mattered most to God. It wasn't material things, or money, or degrees, or even the titles I had garnered. God deems those things insignificant, unimportant. They were the loving things I did from the goodness of my heart that were most important. Until God revealed these to me, I had been completely unaware of them.

I saw myself helping an elderly person with their groceries, comforting a friend in need, saying something kind when others were mean, standing up for the unwanted, advocating for those who couldn't find their voice, and being a patient listener to those who desperately needed to be heard.

It was giving the homeless money when I didn't have money to give and putting others, often complete strangers, first over my own needs because my heart told me it was the right thing to do. It was having a huge heart for all animals, giving love to them, rescuing and caring for them in times of need.

I felt the immediate effect of my words, thoughts and actions  on others. A great majority of these things I did not remember I had done because they were mostly things I did when no one was looking.

But God was looking.

I understood in that moment, that these things were displays of love, kindness, and compassion. They were the only things that mattered in God's eyes. They all required love. Love was the answer to everything!

God placed in my heart the value of the little things, the loving things we did for each other.

By this point, I realized I had only been shown positive things. But I knew I wasn't perfect. My religious upbringing taught me that none of us are without sin. I was a sinner. I believed I had made many, many bad choices and mistakes in my life and if God should have judged anyone, it was me. Yet, God did not show me anything negative. Instead, each time I had a thought or reaction to a scene in my life review, God answered it without judgment.

I was delivered into the hands of God, and I remember waiting and thinking, I haven't been judged yet. I was imperfect! Shouldn't God judge me? Isn't that what I deserve?

On earth, I had been judged by people for making mistakes, not being skinny enough or not wearing the right clothes, just being different from everyone else. I waited to be judged by God. I was sure it was coming. But as I waited to be judged the most unexpected thing happened. God, once again, began to fill me with unconditional love.

As his love flowed through me, it washed away any thoughts and feelings of judgment and disappointment. I never felt judged but I should have been judged. Yet He did not judge me. He loved me!

# THE RIPPLING EFFECT

*"I am the light of the world."*

Jesus

I knew at that very moment I never wanted to be separated from God again. I was *Home*. But God wasn't finished with his lessons for me yet. God told me to look to my right. Suddenly, His right arm and shoulder appeared in human form.

They were the size of a semi-truck! I watched Him reach forward and swiftly swing His right arm straight up. It extended to the furthest stars until it was no longer visible. All of a sudden, His hand appeared and resting in His palm was a massive rock. It was bigger than the largest boulder I had ever seen on earth. Emanating from this rock was the most brilliant light.

God turned to me and said, *"You are the rock. You are the Light. The Light is of Me and I AM with you."*

At once, God let loose the rock and together we watched it fall for what felt like a lifetime. I repeated to myself, "I am the Light. I am the rock." As the rock drew near, I saw a vast body of water appear. It was greater than the largest ocean and it stretched so far in every direction that there were no borders. Into the water the rock plunged, and I could feel the great force of its impact. Together we watched as a single ripple of water appeared.

God said, *"Mankind is the water. You are the ripple."* I watched the single ripple expand until I could no longer see it. I repeated, "I am the ripple."

And then God turned to me and said, *"Like the ripple affects the water, so too does man's words and actions affect mankind. You are the rock. You are the light. You are the ripple that affects mankind."*

I began to comprehend its significance. Every word, thought and action, no matter how small, affected everyone and everything. I had no idea of the power and consequences of my thoughts, my words and actions. I knew it was imperative that I remember this if I returned to earth. I had it all wrong! I hadn't given importance to the "little things" and how each of my words, thoughts and actions affected others.

We are all the rock, and the light dwells in each of us if we allow it. This light comes from the one who created us. We have a choice to let that light shine or not. The stronger our connection to God; the brighter the light shines within us.

I could see that I had to start by learning to love myself the way God loved me, and that no one had the qualifications necessary to define me or to take my power. I felt so much peace knowing that, while I am just one person, this love, this light, means that I can make a difference by carefully choosing my thoughts, words, and actions.

Fueled by love, I understood that if we come together with this individual power we carry within, the ripple would be unstoppable. It could change everything.

# GIFTS FROM GOD

*"Your uniqueness is your value, and your value is your*
*contribution on your Earthly Journey."*

Erica McKenzie

A s I tried to wrap my mind around the enormity of this revelation, God asked me to look once again. To my right the stars parted. This time behind the curtain were the most amazing, multidimensional shelves. The shelves reached high into the stars until I could no longer see the tops of them. I looked in front of me past the most distant galaxy and the shelves kept on going. I turned to look behind me, beyond the furthest galaxy, until I could see no farther. The shelves kept on going. I was speechless at the sight of these glorious shelves. These shelves were alive!

On the shelves appeared gifts, presents, like those we give and receive at Christmas. There were so many gifts on all of the shelves that they filled each and every space available. But not one gift looked like the other. Not one was the same.

God said, *"When you are born I give each of you gifts. When you were born, Erica, I gave you the gift of patience and the gift of beauty."*

Immediately I thought *Oh no, God, that can't be right!* I recalled the kids in school. I've been judged all my life. If I were truly beautiful, I wouldn't have been judged. The very events in my life that led up to the day I died happened because I truly felt I wasn't good enough; I wasn't beautiful enough according to mankind's standards.

As feelings of self-doubt and inadequacy filled my being, He so lovingly corrected me by saying telepathically, *"Erica, I gave you the gift of patience and I gave you the gift of beauty."*

I knew in that very moment that the gift of beauty came from within my heart. The gift of beauty was from Him.

God added, *"In life I have more gifts for each and every one of you. All you have to do is ask, and then be prepared to be quiet and listen, to be able to receive these gifts."*

Sometimes it's hard to see the gifts we possess. I thought of my gift of beauty and realized how impossible it was for me to see it in myself because I looked to mankind for my value instead of God. I had stifled the very gifts He had given me. I allowed many of the kids in school and several people throughout my life to make me feel badly about myself. What I came to understand was, as hurtful as they were, they didn't really have the power to take my gifts away. I could finally see. I had the power all along! *It took dying to make me realize that my uniqueness was my value and my value was my contribution on this Earthly Journey.*

As we stood together in silence, God filled me with the knowledge that it was important to share these lessons with others. They applied to each and every one of us. Then God pressed something else upon my heart. I understood it's never about one person using their gifts or uniqueness alone. Rather, it is God's plan for us to embrace our uniqueness and come together to embrace and empower each other. By growing our relationship with each other, side by side, none greater than the other, we are able to go on and accomplish great things. As I studied the gifts on the shelves, I realized not one was the same. It was all so clear. Now I understood why.

Our gifts are different because God designed us to be different. We each have a unique blueprint which is created to provide healing to our body, mind and spirit. Our gifts are also part of our blueprint. So it is our responsibility to be our unique selves because it is the key that will allow us to access our blueprints as we embrace, grow and use these God-given gifts. Then, we come together with our contributions, and to empower and awaken each other. Working together, we go on to do great things.

Suddenly, I knew the secret to unlock these glorious gifts from God.

# A NEW EARTH

*"And we know that for those who love God all things work together for good, for those who are called according to his purpose."*

Romans 8:28 (ESV)

We must be quiet and listen to God. He is the key to help unlock these unique gifts. It is also through our connection with God that we are able to heal our body, mind and spirit. We can grow these gifts and use them in the capacity for which they were designed. When we connect with God, we take our gifts to a whole new level. It all finally made sense!

It is through Love that we will be able to accomplish this. I didn't love and honor my uniqueness because I allowed the thoughts, words and actions of others to dictate how I saw and felt about myself. The more I listened to their words, the harder I worked to change. I did this for so long that I ended up losing my sense of self. My thoughts drifted to the moments before I took my last breath on Earth. Pastor Dan had asked me, "Child, what is your name?" Sadly, I didn't know who I was any more and suddenly this trip to Heaven began to make so much sense to me. Only by truly loving my authentic self could I access my blueprint, my uniqueness, allowing me to heal my life, embrace my gifts from God and my uniqueness. Only then would I be able to fulfill my God-given earthly mission.

Until now, I'd only felt the most overwhelming, unconditional love in the presence of God. Yet now I was overcome by something else, a deep, aching sadness. The only thing on earth I could compare it to would be the death of a child.

While I have never experienced this loss, I can only imagine it would cause such an insurmountable pain that I honestly don't know if I would have the strength to go on. I compared the depth of the pain I was feeling to the death of a child multiplied millions of times over.

It was then that I realized it was coming from God. I just had to know why He felt such deep sadness and pain. As soon as the thought entered my mind, He asked me who in my family believed in Him?

A Rolodex appeared in my mind. As I scrolled through it, the names and faces of family and friends appeared. I thought about everyone in my family who believed in God and strangely, I felt such relief that they did. God motioned towards the stars and there in the distance appeared earth. It was beautiful.

Thoughts of my family, my husband, my friends, classmates, and most of all my children, came to mind. They were still on earth. I instantly knew where they were and that they were safe and happy. And I knew exactly what they were doing.

My children were my greatest gift and the most important thing to me. I loved them beyond measure, but here, in the presence of God, the strangest thing happened. I didn't want to go back to be with them. I wanted to stay in Heaven with God.

Not even the deep love I had for my children could override the overwhelming sense of peace and love I felt in God's presence. I was Home and nothing else mattered. Not even my children because I was given the knowledge that one day we would all be together again and until then they'd be fine. In fact, we are always together. There is a bridge between Heaven and earth. It really does exist.

As I slowly watched the earth spin in the distance, flames began to spread from the bottom of the earth upward. Brilliant orange and yellow flames surrounded earth and shot into space. Terrified, waves of panic swept through me. Nothing would survive the inferno. My family was down there. My children were down there!

"Oh God!" I cried out. "Help them!"

Once again, the glasses appeared. I abruptly turned away and squeezed my eyes shut, filled with dread. The last time I put them on, I could see what I hadn't been able to see before. I didn't want to look through those glasses even though I knew I would gain Heavenly knowledge that only comes from God. I didn't have a choice as my head swung around and the glasses moved towards my face. My hands automatically reached out to guide them to me once again.

Once the glasses were on, I reluctantly opened my eyes. When I did, I gasped, horrified. The earth was completely engulfed in flames. I was helpless to stop it. I didn't want to have this knowledge. Wasn't there someone more qualified who should be seeing this?

As I stared at the scene in front of me, shaken to the core, the clarity of the glasses revealed something I had missed. There, in between the flames, were little streaks of silvery white lights lifting off from every corner of the earth and flying over our heads into Heaven behind us.

At first, there were hundreds, and then thousands upon thousands joined them. They rose from the earth through the flames, unscathed, upward toward our left, and then curved back in our direction, sweeping over our heads on a direct route to Heaven behind us.

The silvery streaks were souls! I will never forget the color of those souls. They were the most luminous white, with a silvery gold coloring woven throughout. There was such strength, beauty and power in the light from each soul.

I recognized their light as the same light in the rock that God had shown me during my lesson on the Rippling Effect. His words echoed in my mind. *"The light is of me and I am with you."*

The *light* gave them the power to lift off the earth and away from the flames. This light acted as a shield that offered protection from the flames that engulfed earth.

I could feel their light. We were all connected, and I have never felt such relief. I knew my family was among them and I knew they were safe. My next thought was for God and His pain.

Pointing towards the earth, I turned to Him and said, "Look, God. It's okay. See? All the souls are safe. I can see them through the flames. They're coming to Heaven."

I felt such joy that all these souls were saved, but God's sadness remained. I couldn't understand my feeling of joy and His of despair. "Why are you still so sad?"

He drew my attention back toward earth. As I looked between the flames, I could see millions of people left behind. Frantic, I turned back to God for an answer.

*"It's free will, Erica."*

"Free will?" I asked.

*"With the gift of life, I give you free will."*

"But why can't you save them? Don't you love them too?"

*"I love all of my children."* God said. *"But I can't make them love me back."*

"Maybe they don't know how," I offered.

*"It's simple,"* God said. *"Love is the connection that joins us together."*

I finally understood why he was so sad and how difficult it must be to love someone so much, yet allow them to make their own choices, even if it caused them pain, even if they were left behind.

The only thing I can compare it to is how I felt as each of my children faced different obstacles and challenges that many times were quite painful. Through it all I had been their voice, their advocate and cheerleader, and supported them in every way possible. I have also been a silent and unwavering force of strength and love they could turn to when needed. Even though I was not able to give myself the same love and support, I came to appreciate everything God was feeling and realized that my unwavering love was the best gift I could give my children.

Eventually, I had to let go of my children as God let go of his, so they could experience life, seek their own opportunities to learn and make their own choices, despite how excruciating it was to see them struggle to find their way. As their parent, I loved them enough to let them to try. I recognized that God also loved His children enough to let them try, despite the pain He felt having to watch those souls perish of their own free will.

I felt a shift in God's energy as He continued. *"There will be a transformation, a new earth, Erica. I have waited patiently and longed for man to find the love in his heart. He has allowed ego, greed and pride to dictate his actions and he has destroyed himself and the earth along with it."*

Turning toward God, I asked, "But what about the animals?" I recognized that as a species we have abused our stewardship, not only of our planet, but of the animals and ourselves as well. But the animals shouldn't have to perish too.

*"Animals are my gift to mankind. They are mankind's greatest earthly teachers of unconditional love,"* said God.

Animals loved us unconditionally just as God does. I've loved cared for animals all my life. They made it easy to feel and show love. I couldn't understand how some people could be so cruel and heartless to helpless creatures. But then again, many people were also heartless and cruel to themselves and to each other.

Loving each other unconditionally was the real challenge. Animals allow us to easily access our heart and feel the unconditional love God has for us. Becoming familiar with that feeling makes it easier to recognize when we truly love others and ourselves unconditionally.

While I watched, the last of the souls left earth. I turned with God toward Heaven and gasped at the remarkable sight in front of me. I have never seen anything so magnificent. Heaven was so huge that earth appeared as a speck of dust in comparison. I watched the souls ascending into Heaven: God's new earth.

Heaven was a planet.

# THE GIFT

*"For the first time, I didn't have to worry about anything other than being who God made me to be."*

Erica McKenzie

I stared longingly at this glorious, golden planet and knew it was exactly where I belonged: a place filled with love and peace. My heart longed to be where unconditional love reigned and we all shared a connection with God.

Together God and I shared a lifetime of lessons. On earth, we measure everything by time, but the unusual thing about Planet Heaven was that time didn't exist. I just knew I was staying in Heaven. I never wanted to be parted from God again.

I hadn't considered the possibility of going back. I knew if I returned I would face the toughest battle of all—learning to love myself like God loved me. But standing in His presence and feeling His unconditional love made it easy to love myself. What was the point of having to do it on earth when I was able to do it here?

God answered my thoughts. *"Erica, until you learn to love yourself, you will be unable to fulfill your earthly mission. You will be unable to heal and grow the gifts I have given you."*

Without having love for myself, I had become broken and lost. My mind drifted to the hotel when Jesus said, "Come" and I chose to follow him to the correct room. He knew the way.

This was why God sent Jesus for me to follow him that day. Jesus is love and love is the way to reconnect with God. I was not forced – I chose of my own free-will to follow him. Suddenly, I was filled with peace and the knowledge that God would never leave me no matter what I experienced on earth. But I still had no intention of returning to earth.

God continued, *"I was with you throughout your life, as I was the moments before your death, when you heard my voice and made the choice of faith. You trusted in me and my wisdom when you could have chosen mankind's voice."*

Now I understood why I suddenly believed that Jesus, the man who helped me at the hotel, was a terrorist and that he had a bomb. It was a powerful human catalyst for action. Listening to God was the faith choice and I immediately realized why it was so important that I ran when God told me to run. Jesus told me to "take rest," not take a bath. Had I gotten in the bathtub, my body would have died right then, leaving my spirit without the ability to return to my body and complete my earthly mission. God told me to run to save my life. Just then my revelation was interrupted by God.

*"It is time,"* God said. *"I have two more gifts to give you. I am giving you the gift of knowledge and the gift of wisdom."*

As I stood in the presence of God, I felt him surround me and fill me with answers that came faster than my questions. I was overwhelmed at the rate with which I received the knowledge. The extent of this knowledge was downloaded in enormous volumes of information. It was telepathy on steroids.

My initial reaction to this huge transfer of data was laughter mixed with my excitement. One may think that's an inappropriate response, but God laughed with me because He understood. We both thought about Shane Martin's head and how I tried to rub it as a child, believing that somehow Shane's "smarts" would rub off on me.

God knew my heart and that those actions were a reflection of the love, admiration and appreciation I had for Shane's gift. Now, I was instantly filled with the knowledge of the Universe. If learning on earth had only been that simple...

I thought about my upbringing and how religion was used as a tool to help increase my knowledge. I was thankful for that tool and yet I didn't feel the importance of religion to God.

God was much bigger than religion. Religion had actually placed God in a box. The truth was our love for God was most important and it was the personal relationship with our Creator that mattered, not the religion within which we found him.

God is love and we serve God when we love ourselves and we love each other. It is through this loving relationship that we are able to empower one another. When we love ourselves, we can finally come to a place where we no longer focus on our imperfections, but instead, focus on our gifts.

I had focused on my imperfections my entire life. These same imperfections would bring me my greatest spiritual growth. In fact, for the first time, I could really see how I had it all backwards. I realized that I had tried to change myself to become worthy when I was already valuable in God's eyes. How could I be myself once more? To love myself is not to judge myself – it is to forgive myself and it is where I will find myself.

My heart swelled to bursting with love for God. "Thank you for all of the lessons you so patiently taught me." I now understood that all of the focus and energy I put into changing to meet mankind's standards was the very roadblock that kept me from completing my earthly mission. It kept me from connecting with God and hearing His voice, and it stifled my ability to move forward on my journey.

The more I dwelled on this desire to change myself to meet mankind's expectations, the more challenging it became to identify my gifts from God. This then made it impossible to grow my gifts and empower myself and others. What I needed was to embrace love and appreciation for myself and *dare to be me*. Only when I could truly be myself would I be able to discover my true value and heal my life.

God knew exactly what he was doing when he made me and the sooner I realized this the sooner I'd be able to heal, creating a sense of balance between my body, mind and spirit. Creating this balance is only achieved when we love ourselves and then acknowledge and grow our unique gifts. Without loving myself first, I'd never be able to go on to truly love or help others on the level that God had planned for me. For the first time, I felt as if I didn't need to worry about anything other than being who God made me to be. It was such a sense of relief to feel that I was good enough and to believe it with my heart.

God made it clear He had a plan for everyone and that we are not to judge someone else's journey. There is no love present where judgment is. We are to love others, the way God made them, not the way we desire for them to be. To love is to forgive. We are here to help each other. Our experiences, even the most tragic and painful, are opportunities to remain in the state of love, grow our compassion and kindness, and maintain our connection to God. It all finally made sense. It was so simple and I wondered why I didn't get it while I was on earth. I was so glad I was staying in Heaven!

I felt God smile and then He said, *"You're not staying child. I'm sending you back because your mission has just begun. You work for me now, remember? And Erica, when you go back, you must be quiet and listen to the people I put into your life. Then when you do, you will take patience, beauty, and now knowledge and wisdom, and when you speak you will change millions of lives."*

The contract I had made with God on that fateful plane ride home to Kansas City came to mind. But I had absolutely no intention of going back. I couldn't bring myself to consider the very thought of being parted from God again, from my true home! In the instant it took for the first thoughts to form to argue my case to stay on Planet Heaven, I felt myself drawn into a tunnel of total darkness.

# THE EDGE OF HELL

*"I have come into the world as light, so that whoever believes in me may not remain in darkness."*

John 12:46 (ESV)

A dark and empty void surrounded me. My arms were pressed tightly against my sides as I slowly moved downward through a constrictive tunnel. This time the tunnel was very different. I had no ability to use my senses. I couldn't see or hear anything. This was nothing like the tunnel filled with love and light that I had traveled through to Heaven. I was terrified.

One moment I stood with God and the next, I was utterly, irrevocably alone. The absence of His unconditional love was obvious. This was Hell.

As I strained to feel, hear or see something, anything, from my left ear I heard a faint buzzing sound. Focusing all my energy on the white noise, I heard it grow louder and suddenly my downward movement stopped. One moment I was vertical in the tunnel, and the next I was horizontal, paralyzed, and moving sideways away from the tunnel and toward the noise.

Part of me was relieved to hear something; to feel as if I wasn't alone. The more I strained to hear the muffled noise, the more I moved toward it. Again, I was relieved because at least I was going somewhere. My hearing was the only one of my senses working. I was determined to use my sense of hearing to get help and figure out how to get myself back to earth. The muffled sound became a murmur. The sound was human and I recognized the din of voices, which sounded as if I was in a convention center with thousands of people.

The voices were of all nationalities, all speaking different languages. As I strained to hear their conversations, I realized that I was able to understand all of the different conversations at the same time. Growing up in a small town, we had not been given the opportunity to learn a foreign language, yet I understood what each person was saying. There were thousands upon thousands of conversations occurring at once and they were all negative. They were criticizing and judging each other. There were angry and jealous conversations, full of gossip and spitefulness. These conversations were the exact opposite of the unconditional love and acceptance that emanated from God.

Along with the conversations came the feelings those thoughts and words produced. They were the most extreme emotions of sadness, anger, hatred, loneliness, jealousy, self-loathing, unworthiness and everything you can imagine that was negative. I didn't want to feel those overwhelming emotions but they washed over me like a tidal wave. This destructive energy was delivered to me all at once by all those different people. It was so strong it drained me of my life force, my God-light. Those people were unaware of my presence, just as they were unaware of the effect of their extreme negativity on me.

Paralyzed, I lay on my back hovering just above them. I could neither see nor speak, and realized instantly that I was suspended at the Edge of Hell. The moment I recognized Hell, the souls in Hell recognized me. They could see my light and were drawn to it. I was beyond terrified. I can't even find a human word to explain the degree of sheer terror I felt. Part of that terror was due to the realization that mine was the only light in that entire place.

How could this be? That realization created an energy or force and suddenly I could feel hands touching me everywhere. I could feel their fingerprints and fingers, whether it was a pinky or thumb, pressing into my flesh. There were little hands and big hands, young hands and old hands. They were pawing and groping me. They were pulling me toward Hell.

The sense of helplessness was overwhelming. It's impossible to describe the scale of the sensations. Everything in the world of spirit seems magnified a thousand times over. Everything in the world of Spirit also brings a level of clarity that is impossible to achieve in our earthly realm and human form. As they touched me, they pulled me down, literally sucking out my life force. My light grew dimmer and I panicked. I knew I wasn't going to get out of there. I was a fuel station, a light for them. They had stifled their own light. They put their own life force out and now they wanted mine!

Love created the light. God said, *"You are the light, the light is of Me and I am with you."* He was with me always—not sometimes and not in some places, but always. I realized that a love connection with God created the light and the stronger the connection, the brighter the light. People on earth would need this light to shine in the tunnel to find their way home to God and Heaven. Without it, they would never find their way back. They'd be stuck in Hell. The only thing I could do was to cry out, "Help me, God! Why am I here? Please help me! I love you!"

My voice and words created power and the hands reluctantly lifted off me, yet this process seemed to take forever. I kept crying out to God, professing my love for Him. When I finally became free of all the hands, God propelled me away from the reach of those souls trapped in Hell.

Still lying on my back with my hands pressed to my sides, unable to move, I began to lift up and float to the right, away from Hell. As I did, I began to cry for those people. *These poor people!* I thought. Despite all their negativity and the desperation to help themselves at my expense, I still wanted to save them.

"God, please let me help them!" I knew that with God, all things were possible. And then I remembered that God gives each of us the gift of free will. They had a choice. It was up to them to save themselves.

With a heavy heart, I will try to accurately describe the magnitude of deep sadness I felt as I began to drift forward, leaving those poor people behind. Can you imagine being somewhere so horrific, so terrible, and where you feel so alone and powerless? Then a glimmer of hope rescues you from that tragedy.

An overwhelming sense of relief flooded me. I was so grateful for my escape, and yet at the same time I couldn't bear to leave those people. I didn't want to go and yet I understood I couldn't stay as my own free will would not allow it. I was humbled because I had never known this type of ultimate choice at this level until I was given the opportunity to experience it in Hell.

I could hear my labored breath as I continued to drift. Eventually I came to a familiar place. It was the tunnel where I had come to a stop. I was gently moved from lying on my back, face up to Heaven, to standing on my feet, my hands still fixed to my sides. I still didn't have any voluntary movement. This tunnel was my vehicle back to earth and it was the connection to God that saved me.

I continued to cry out to God and was instantly downloaded with information. God wanted me to see and understand the magnitude of what He was trying to explain in Heaven. It was about having the courage to value my uniqueness and not to judge or put someone down, but to come together to empower others. He needed me to experience the destructive nature of words, thoughts and actions and how we can easily be influenced by the negative energy and forces they create.

I am a kinesthetic learner, which means I learn by doing. I realized that God sent me there to actually experience this lesson. It wasn't to test me but to drive home the point He was trying to make. I had to *feel* it. I had to experience it, so that when I returned to earth I would have the courage and conviction to convey the message because I had lived it.

God loves us unconditionally, but I realized it's our love connection with Him that is most important. God cannot do it for us; we cannot do it for another, we each have to do it for ourselves. It is "the work." He wasn't punishing us. It was another example of our free will.

I received the knowledge that God did not put those people there. They put themselves there by choosing separation from God and His love. With the gift of free will, they chose separation from Him. After the unconditional love I felt from God, why would anyone want to be separate from it? God explained to me that there was no time limit or expiration date on His gift of free will. All of the people in Hell had the ability to get out at any time.

Getting out may sound quite simple to you and me because it's as simple as choosing to love God. A feeling of love from them to God would simply be enough to turn that light on within and free themselves of that terrible place. They chose not to have the connection to God for whatever reason. They alone were the ones who closed the connection. When God showed me the souls lifting off the earth in flames, He said to me, *"Erica, it's free will."*

The reality was I had to learn and understand what free will really meant, and going to Hell did it. When we choose to have a connection with God, He respects it because He sees our hearts. He is only looking for love, not perfection. Love is the only answer.

Anger, jealousy, hatred, spitefulness, gossip, self- loathing, unworthiness, guilt and judgment are all elements of negative energy. They are the antithesis of God's unconditional love. It was beyond my power to save those people. I felt such great sadness for them and wanted to help them all but they had to save themselves. I witnessed what God meant by free will. I was exercising my choice of free will by choosing to have a connection with God. I experienced God's power when I cried out for Him to save me.

We are each on our own unique journey and there are times when we know the answer for other people but realize they are not ready to hear it. The desire and need must come from within them. They must initiate the connection to God and His love. Once again, I felt the depth of God's sadness knowing He had to allow those souls to disconnect from Him. I had to leave those people behind. I realized I only had the power to save myself. I could only be responsible for me.

It was difficult to leave them behind even though they had stifled their own connection. They had become their own roadblock. They were the only ones who could reconnect to God. In order to do so, they'd have to move past their egos in order to understand, to reflect, to be quiet and listen, and to reestablish the connection to God. They would have to find love within themselves. No matter how many people prayed for them, it was still up to each individual to free himself from Hell. "It was doing the work."

As I moved back into the tunnel to return to earth, I knew I had to continue to talk to God. I could not break that connection. "Thank you, God. I love you, God. I work for you, God." As I talked to Him, I was filled with unconditional love. I was the vehicle. The unconditional love from God was the fuel that sustained me for my trip to earth. It moved me forward and the more I called out and talked to God, the closer I moved toward earth.

The journey back was a dark, confining, cumbersome and tedious process. I was beyond exhausted. I couldn't breathe. When I focused on drawing a breath, it broke the connection. The minute I closed my connection to God I would come to a complete stop, hear that buzzing noise and begin to move out of the tunnel toward the Edge of Hell. I knew if I moved back to that place on the Edge of Hell, they would suck the life force out of me and this time I wouldn't have the energy to cry out. I would never escape. I could not take my focus off God, not even to breathe.

# BACK TO EARTH

*"For those who believe, there are no words needed. For those who do not believe, there are no words possible."*

Saint Ignatius of Loyola

Once again, I cried out to God. I continued to talk to him. I didn't breathe. I didn't think. I didn't do anything but talk to God. Though it was extremely taxing, I did it because having that connection was all that mattered. It really was enough to sustain me. It felt like it took another lifetime to return to earth, but eventually I made it.

Floating near the ceiling of the emergency room, I found myself staring at my husband, Derek. He was sitting in a chair with his head resting on my limp body. His eyes were red from crying and I could feel his great sadness and exhaustion.

It was my body but I also knew the real me was not attached to that body. I honestly didn't think I could shove myself back into what had once felt so familiar, but now I identified as foreign. I knew reintegrating was going to be overwhelming and painful. That body wasn't me!

I was limitless, powerful, filled with God's love and light. I carried the knowledge of the Universe. I carried God's message and lessons. I was a spiritual being, not that limp, worn out, abused body on the gurney. It was too confining and claustrophobic to even consider trying to stuff myself inside it. There must be another solution, but I couldn't think of one.

*Please God, don't make me do it. I can't! There must be another way I can come back and do this work for you.*

Those thoughts had barely formed in my head when I was sucked to the ceiling by what felt like a giant magnet. I moved helplessly across the ceiling, over the top of the curtained partition that separated the emergency bays and was then unceremoniously planted on my butt on a gurney.

Three kind, elderly nurses appeared in front of me. They wore scrubs, but also a glowing aura of light around each of them. There were no wings, but I knew they were angels here to counsel me, sent by God.

"Be quiet and listen," one of them said. "You will go back into your body. You work for God now, remember? You have received your assignment to complete your earthly mission."

A second one spoke, "It's going to be painful and your obstacles will be great. Few will be easy and none will be without effort to overcome. Remember your gifts."

The third one said, "Child, your uniqueness is your value and your value is your contribution on this Earthly Journey."

There was no negotiating. I didn't have a choice. As soon as they finished telling me these things, I had to re-enter my body. I felt the giant magnet suck me back to the ceiling. The three angels disappeared beneath me and vanished into the light. My heart sank. I had always known them too. I would miss them.

Most of all I would miss God.

I slid back over the curtain, what I knew to be the very veil that separates us from the Heavens, and into the room with Derek and my body. As I looked down on myself, I realized I couldn't do this. But again, I heard the voice. *"You are the rock. You are the light. The light is of me and I am with you, child."* It was God. My heart burst with an ache and longing so deep I would have done anything to be with Him again.

In a split second, I was shoved back into my limp body like a hand in a glove, only the glove was too small.

Each part of my spiritual body squeezed its way into my physical counterpart. I could feel my spiritual big toe fit back into the spot of my physical big toe along with each one of my fingers, my hands, feet, arms and legs.

My body felt heavy and confined as if I'd been zipped inside a jacket two sizes too small. All the feelings attached to my sick and exhausted body assaulted my spiritual one. My chest hurt along with the rest of me. This was an enormous let down from the light-filled vastness of Spirit I had just experienced.

It wasn't me at all! I had lived as a multidimensional being, basking in the love of God's presence only to be forced back into the stark reality of a 3-dimentional body. How could I possibly go back to that?

All these emotions and thoughts swirled through me as I woke. My body felt dense and foreign. My throat burned. Waves of exhaustion crashed over me as I regained consciousness. I forced my eyes open and began to look around the room. There was a partitioned curtain wall on each side of me. Looking down, I noticed I was positioned on my back on that gurney and I was still in the emergency room. Derek was sitting in a chair to my left. I let out a deep breath that caught his attention. I looked into his eyes and tried to speak to tell Derek where I had been.

But I didn't have a voice!

Derek looked at me in disbelief. "Oh my God, Erica, what the hell happened?"

I needed to tell him where I'd been but nothing would come out! He continued, frustrated yet relieved at the same time. "I tried calling you over and over, but you didn't answer. I tried the Holiday Inn, but you hadn't checked in like I told you to. I was so worried that I called the police and they said suggested checking credit cards, ATM withdrawals and the hospitals because it was too soon to file a missing persons report."

My mind reeled with this information as I tried to recall all that had happened. But it was trivial. I'd been to Planet Heaven! I wanted desperately to shout it to the world.

"When I finally tracked you to the other hotel, you had vanished. The police called and said they had a Jane Doe that matched your description at the hospital."

All I heard was blah, blah, blah. I had been to Heaven! I had talked with God! I opened my mouth to tell my husband, but I still had no voice.

The emergency room staff appeared and checked my vital signs. The emergency room physician added, "We're going to admit you to the hospital overnight so that you can rest and we can ensure that you are okay." Once again, I tried to speak but nothing came out; I was too exhausted to even try. I only remember drifting in and out of consciousness, but I don't remember much more of what my husband or the staff said to me. The next time I woke, I glanced around at the sterile room and the empty bed next to me. I had never felt so alone.

I didn't know how much time had passed. What I did know, as a nurse, was that the doctors made their first rounds in the morning. Groggy and exhausted, I didn't feel good. Desperately trying to make sense of my trip to Planet Heaven, I didn't recognize the doctor who walked into my hospital room.

"Mrs. McKenzie, how are you this morning? I'm Dr. Imanass."

My stomach cramped. Oh God, here it comes! Like a gushing unexpected wave, I was going to throw up. I reached for the pink bedpan to catch my vomit. But then I realized it wasn't vomit coming up. It was my voice. I was throwing up my voice.

"Doctor, Doctor, Oh my God! I have to tell you where I just came from!"

It was God who gave me the words as they flew out of my mouth. I had no control over what came out of me. I felt as if I were watching a movie and observing the unfolding drama. "I've just been to Heaven. I talked with God and He showed me so many things."

Dr. Imanass cut me off immediately, turned and hurried out of the room. He didn't acknowledge one word I said. He didn't even complete my needed health assessment. It was as if I had the plague and he couldn't risk another minute in my presence for fear he would either catch what I had or, worse yet, perish.

I'd just been to Heaven, Hell and back and the first person I told couldn't run away fast enough. A doctor is supposed to help you. What had I done wrong?

The door to my room was still ajar and a nurse who'd been standing in the hallway charting on her patients, peeked inside. Her warm smile lit her compassionate eyes. She quietly crossed the room and sat down on the edge of my bed. The years had etched themselves in lines that gathered in the corners of her mouth. As she leaned in toward me, she pressed her finger to her lips.

"Shhh...Be quiet and listen," she whispered. "I heard what you said. I believe you, but you must listen to me carefully because I need you to hear my words. I've worked for that doctor for seven years and that man is an atheist. I'm so sorry that the first person you told your experience to about God was someone who doesn't believe in God."

Her voice was gentle and encouraging and I listened carefully as she spoke. I remembered what God had said to me in Heaven. "Erica, be quiet and listen to the people I put in your life." The nurse had spoken the same words God had admonished to me—*Be quiet and listen.*

I can't tell you how many times I was told to be quiet and listen throughout my entire experience. I would later come to understand that it was a lesson not just for me but for us all.

She had tears in her eyes as she continued. "I believe in God, but now is not the time to tell your story. I could get fired for even discussing it with you. Once you leave here, don't stop telling your story. You'll know when it's time. It's important to share it."

I knew she was afraid for her job and she was helping me at great personal risk. The instant she said it, I received a download from God.

I was on the psych ward.

# HELL ON EARTH

*"In Heaven, I was handed a pair of eye glasses. God said, "Now look." For the first time in my life I could see."*

Erica McKenzie

Flooded with memories from nursing school, I remembered the rotation I had on the psych ward as a nursing student. It was one of the more difficult things I've done. I felt like the patients there were forgotten people. My instructor said it was important to appear attentive and to act as if you were listening. "Mental health care provides people the opportunity to lead a normal life like everyone else, and these people are not normal," she stated.

She also said not to believe what the patients were saying because they were not speaking truth, but merely attempting to manipulate. I knew it was wrong in nursing school and didn't understand how some people could be so cruel. I was told they were crazy. Yet several of them appeared to have the ability to communicate with something we couldn't see. I felt that many of them were medicated because of it. It was horrible.

I grew up believing that the purpose of medicine was to heal the sick, not to turn people into something they were not. Here I was, years later, in the exact same position as some of those patients, being dismissed and medicated because I had an experience the doctor couldn't explain.

I'll admit running from a hotel thinking a bomb was about to go off isn't the type of dinner conversation one would expect to hear about without raising eyebrows. Yet, I cannot dismiss the strange and synchronistic events of my experience or the Voice of God, which I had heard since childhood, that directed my steps when my physical body was failing. Call what I did crazy if you must – you won't hear me contest it. But what did being crazy really mean? And did it constitute a solution if the cure came in the form of a pill? Maybe I was just broken and lost.

I realized through my own experience that those patients needed to be heard by an educated, empathetic and caring staff. I couldn't help but feel that the majority of the drugs administered to many of these patients acted as a Band-aid, only able to reduce or mask the symptoms temporarily, if they were therapeutic at all. I sensed the drugs affected the ability of several of the patients to think clearly. Even more terrifying, I sensed the drugs were changing those people and I'm certain in some cases they actually blocked communication to God.

It was a crash course in mental health care, starting with my perceived "crazy behavior and delusions." I learned in nursing school that medication was the most "therapeutic" way to treat "crazy behavior and delusions."

Now the tables were turned. I realized it was a multidimensional lesson. Everything that happened to me up until the day I died, including my trip to Heaven, Hell and the psych ward, was preparing me to help myself and others. That help would include educating the medical community about near-death experiences, the presence of God and our ability to connect with our Creator, as a miracle, not a medical issue. In fact, those miracles would provide great healing.

I later learned that my trip to Heaven was called a near-death experience or NDE (http://ndestories.org/). During my NDE, I learned that we are spiritual beings having a human experience. I can't imagine the countless individuals who have experienced spiritual events and have been medicated and dismissed because of it. When does communicating with the unseen or spiritual realm validate a diagnosis of psychosis? It appears society, and especially the medical community, is in dire need of education on NDE's from a spiritual level. The effect of doing so would have the potential to increase their receptiveness and support of their patients' experiences and could assist in distinguishing the psychic from the psychotic.

While there are people who have hallucinations and need certain treatments and pharmacological therapies to function well and live healthy lives, NDE's should not necessarily be grouped in with such hallucinations and neither should people who were simply broken.

I felt strongly that the system, as a whole, was abusing the privilege of prescribing medications. According to wikipedia.org, a therapeutic effect is a consequence of a medical treatment of any kind, the results of which are judged to be desirable and beneficial. This is true whether the result was expected, unexpected, or even when there are unintended consequences of the treatment.

My NDE allowed me to understand the true meaning of the word "judged." God had me wear those glasses in Heaven to allow me to see what I was unable to see on my own. I thought about how humans invented their own type of glasses that raised "normal" vision to 20/20, which was a man-made method of improving the human condition. In that moment, I realized that God sent me back to earth with those glasses with the intention of also improving the human condition. The glasses were now a part of me. I could see many things, and one of them was that the medical system was clearly broken.

Near-death experiences have been documented for years and are rather universal among people who've come close to death. Yet, the subject wasn't addressed during my medical training as a student and I was discouraged to discuss it with patients when I practiced as a hospice nurse.

Listening with understanding, and accessing a component of spiritual knowledge when caring for the patient seems to be lacking from our medical system. Health care professionals are taught not to cross the line into religion, but in my opinion, this type of experience doesn't come under the scope of religion. Several high profile doctors have also had near-death experiences and encountered realms of higher consciousness including God, Jesus, and Archangels. The doctors' near-death experiences radically altered their view of life after death.

A growing scientific community now believes consciousness survives the death of the physical body and near-death experiences are real events. NDE's are as unique as we are. However there is a single common thread through all of them; they are happening around the world to humans of every race, and religion, including atheists and agnostics. Unity, not division, is a vital lesson to take from these experiences.

In medical school, they taught me to be quiet and listen— but not really because I felt this type of listening included judgment of the patient. I felt this judgment stood in the way of really listening to the patient and implementing a treatment plan that would first do no harm. Too many times, the quick answer was medication, not listening with an open mind to possibly discover an alternative diagnosis.

## The Game Changer

My NDE gave me the absolute clarity that human beings consist of two separate parts; the physical body and the spirit. Our minds are the key that link the two together. This is why there is such significance when referring to the body, mind and spirit. Notice that "mind" is in the middle of body and spirit. Be careful not to assume that the mind and the brain, while exceedingly intricate, are one and the same, because my NDE taught me that, while each is important, they are very different.

The brain sides with the body and the mind sides with the spirit. The mind encapsulates and flows freely throughout the limited compartments of the brain. In fact, they each have very different jobs which are both vital components to sustain authentic human life. The brain and the physical organ called the heart work together to sustain physical life as the blood flows in and out through the heart, circulates through our body and brain. It is quite miraculous when we think about it. Then there is our spiritual heart, and some people believe that this is where our soul is kept. The mind and our spiritual heart work together to sustain spiritual life. Like the blood that flows through our bodies and passes in and out of the heart and on to the brain, so too does our spiritual blood flow through our spiritual bodies, passing in and out of our spiritual heart and on to our minds.

We have man-made methods such as glasses and pacemakers that are incredible tools to improve the human condition in the brain and body, but we also have God-made methods like the glasses I was given in Heaven that are tools used to improve the human condition. And humans can only access those methods through their minds and spirits. I came to understand the foundation of this during my NDE and to recognize it as part of our uniquely vital blueprints that sustain authentic life as human beings.

It is imperative that we acknowledge and comprehend that all blueprints are unique. We must learn to access this unique blueprint when addressing and treating each component together to achieve healing. Therefore, it makes sense that the true definition of a therapeutic effect is a consequence of medical treatment of any kind, the results of which are determined through addressing all unique components of body and brain, along with the mind and spirit, which together determines the desirable and beneficial outcome.

There is also a need to identify "medical treatment." I feel that there are numerous effective treatment modalities that deserved to be used when found appropriate. One of those medical treatments, I believe, is an NDE.

Why weren't they teaching this in medical school? The bigger question became why weren't they teaching the spiritual component in medical school? Not only is the NDE one of the effective medical treatments, it is a tool, it is medicine. How were we supposed to fully access and use tools like NDE's for healing if we were not fluent in our knowledge of the Spirit? Millions of people all over the world have reported having them. Did anyone ever stop to question why? Could it be possible that the mind and spirit together, using tools like NDE's, contained knowledge that could aide in improving the human condition and be the key to possibly saving the next step, the next stage of our humanity? After all, when all humans take their last breath and die, they leave their physical bodies behind and it is only their souls that will be allowed to continue the journey.

We attempt to prolong our lifespan by addressing the needs and taking care of our physical body. That being the case, wouldn't you think it important to address and nourish and care for the spiritual component in an effort to keep it as healthy as possible throughout our earthly lifespan and for the journey that lies ahead when we depart?

I'm not passing judgment on any institution or medical professional. That's not why I was sent back. Instead, I am identifying through my experiences and lessons learned, that there is a dire need for education on this subject. Could you imagine being told by your doctor that your heart needs a pacemaker in order to sustain quality of life? The day of surgery you are in the operating room, all prepped and ready to go. The doctor who will be performing your procedure comes in and tells you, "By the way, I'm not familiar with how the pacemaker actually works and I have no knowledge of how to implant it into your body or place it into your heart." You assumed the doctor was competent and armed with the most current knowledge and skills for this procedure. I wonder how many of us would still feel comfortable going under the knife after having a conversation like this?

The lack of knowledge on the doctor's part would clearly indicate a need for more education in order to perform the procedure correctly, thus producing effective results that would move you in the direction of healing your body, not hurting it. Because of this lack of mind/spirit education in the medical community, talking about my trip to Heaven, Hell and God would get me forcibly drugged. Those drugs began to change me, not heal me, because they were not the appropriate medical treatment modality. Yet, what I experienced was real. It happened. My NDE was important because it was a vital component to my healing. I was broken and in this case, it was the medicine I needed.

I was so upset and tried to tell Derek but at this point, he didn't believe me. Derek had been given the nutshell version of the events by the paramedics that unfolded prior to my being transferred to the care of the emergency room staff.

When I think about the magnitude of my story, I guess it would be difficult for anyone to believe it. Especially when everyone was only getting pieces of the events that unfolded, which left room for open interpretation, forcing the brain to fill the gaps with their own beliefs and assumptions.

According to Dr. Imanass, despite the physiologic complications experienced with my lungs and heart, the events leading up to my collapse at the church all pointed to acute mania due to bipolar disorder. When I demanded that he call Dr. Enabler, the doctor who had prescribed the medications to me, he refused and completely dismissed me. He diagnosed my trip to Planet Heaven, Hell and lessons with God as psychosis instead of a near-death experience. Yet a simple phone call to my weight loss doctor, a clinical review of the side-effects of the drugs I was taking, and a call to the pastor to hear his description of the bulging vein in my neck, which occurred moments before I fell unconscious, would have helped to rectify the situation. They would have given credence to my claim that something other than the typical diagnosis of bipolar was happening. It would have helped to differentiate between a physiological problem and a mental one.

Derek was upset because the doctors told him they couldn't help me. They said I was being defiant by refusing to actively participate in group therapy sessions and not talking to the very staff who would medicate me to shut me up.

Of course, I wasn't going to talk! He didn't understand what had really happened because I'd kept my drug use secret. I knew my symptoms were entirely due to the diet medications I had abused for so long. I also knew how some of the medical establishments handled "delusional patients." If I told the truth about my experience, I would risk being medicated until I became compliant. Those medications would change me, and I didn't need to change. I needed to remember who I was and fix my brokenness.

I was in desperate need of receiving the medical treatment called detox. I needed to detox my body, mind and spirit from several years of drug use, but the arrogant doctor allowed his personal feelings to dictate the plan of care for his patient. Derek had no idea the hell I was about to go through.

I couldn't believe it! I'd done such a good job of hiding my drug addiction that no one could imagine my behavior, the increased activity level, loss of appetite, mood swings, random manic episodes and decreased need for sleep, were all drug-induced. It would have also explained my breathing problems. In fact, it would have been simple for the doctor to verify my nearly nine-year prescription to the drugs. But he refused to listen and the consequences of that choice put me at risk. To him I was just another crazy, non-compliant patient who had no idea what she was talking about.

I begged Dr. Imanass and his staff to contact Dr. Enabler. They finally promised me they would. I was certain that the same professional who was so attentive and caring toward me would walk through that psych unit door at any moment on a mission to rescue me from my predicament by validating my claims and declaring responsibility for some of the damage that had been done to my body.

But the hours quickly turned to days as the staff continued to administer the long list of new medications despite my plea. With the medications came suicidal and racing thoughts, night terrors and dizziness. I was shaking and pacing uncontrollably. I could barely function. I kept waiting, hoping Dr. Enabler would come, but she never did. I thought about the prescription diet pills. Dr. Enabler was more than happy to write and dispense to me well beyond the therapeutic time frame. I asked myself, "Why did she do it?" The answer came in the form of another question, "Why did I do it?" Why did I feel compelled to take a drug that I didn't need? I wasn't overweight.

A week went by and I was still refusing to cooperate with the staff or to actively participate in group therapy. Dr. Imanass told Derek not to give up because there was another option. One of the best programs in the country for "my condition" had an opening. Despite being out of state and miles away from home, they had reserved a bed for me. Therefore, against my will, they initiated the patient discharge process, implementing the plans to transfer me to the out-of-state psychiatric hospital.

Derek said, "I have no choice, Erica. You need to get better and the doctor knows best."

Desperate and alone, I was compelled to confront Dr. Imanass once more. "I want help, I'm broken but sending me to another place like this isn't going to help me. Let me detox and stop medicating me just because I tried to tell you about my experience in Heaven," I insisted. He stiffened and stood emotionless.

"Nurse," he called out as he waved his hand to summon her.

The nurse approached me holding a syringe. Oh God, not again, I thought. By this time, I had become familiar with those horrible shots. They completely knocked me out within seconds and would keep me sedated for hours. She administered the shot and I was helpless to stop her. The room began to spin and my vision blurred as I watched the doctor leave the room. He and I both knew I did not have Bipolar disorder but maybe he was just trying to use the drugs to improve my psychological condition in the absence of a true clinical disorder. Or perhaps his actions stemmed from what he was taught in school coupled with his personal belief system.

In 2012 when I returned to the Kansas Hospital for a copy of my medical records for the purpose of this book, they had disappeared. At that time, my request was within the state's legal time frame to hold on to patient medical records, yet they had vanished; except for a short, single page generic record from the paramedics showing patient transfer from ambulance to my admittance to the emergency room. There were no records found showing I was ever in the ER, no details of the actual emergency room visit or for admission from the ER to the psychiatric hospital or record of the seven days spent there. There were no dates, details, or duration of the time I was a patient at that hospital.

Of course, there were multiple credible witnesses who could verify I was admitted to the ER and went on to spend seven days in that hospital, on their psych unit before being transferred out of state.

The clerk who tried to help me was baffled. She apologetically said that in twenty-five years she had worked there, this was the first time she'd been unable to locate a patient's records. I'd been admitted a few times to the same hospital before my NDE in October, 2002 and in the years following for various health issues and all of those records were still available. How does this happen? Why did it happen? Is it possible someone in the hospital conveniently removed my records when I mentioned the high profile doctor who wrote my drug prescriptions?

Years later I found out that not only was Dr. Enabler investigated by the FBI during the period of time I was a patient, but the investigation led to having the privilege of practicing medicine revoked by the state of Kansas. There would be no reason whatsoever for my records to go missing and I have to wonder if this isn't somehow related. My case could have been used as evidence against the doctor before a medical board.

In the meantime, I wanted to scream in frustration. No one was listening to me! I was being committed when I should have been detoxed. I had returned to hell.

# I AM THE ROCK

*"Rejoice not over me, O my enemy; when I fall, I shall rise; when
I sit in darkness, the Lord will be a light to me."*

Micah 7:8 (ESV)

Once committed to the new psych hospital, a nurse accompanied me to my assigned single room. I began to unpack the few items I was allowed to bring, and amongst the items was a letter from Derek.

Erica,

I want you to know that we all love you very much and we're counting the days until you get better and can come home. You should always know that you have my unconditional love and that you mean more to me than you can ever imagine. Feel better and get plenty of rest. The kids are doing better than any of the adults. They know their mommy is in good hands and that you will come home someday soon better than ever. I love you with all my heart! Things will get better and life will change for the best. This is the vacation you've always needed. Take advantage of this special opportunity. I miss you.

Love,
Derek

Upon reading the letter I realized that I was going to remain away from the people I loved the most until I was able to clearly demonstrate I was better. It didn't matter what I thought – at this point detox was no longer an option. I was forced to participate in group therapy like I had done during my stay at the hospital in Kansas. This time I convinced myself that by making an effort I would get closer to being able to return home to my family.

At the new hospital, the staff would make us feel safe so that we could talk about our experiences. In a moment of weakness, coupled with the prescription drugs I was forced to take, I opened up and talked about what had happened to me. I convinced myself I was in a new environment so I had to try because not all health care professionals were the same and maybe one of them would believe me.

And what did they do? They increased the dosage of my meds until I couldn't function. I learned after testing the water a few times not to speak of anything about God or communicating with Spirit because, if I did, it meant I was schizophrenic or bipolar or having delusions. I've never felt so powerless. I was drugged, kept away from my babies for nearly a month, and made to feel I was crazy.

Is this how our medical industry is trained? My heart sank. I was in such despair. There were times throughout the day that we had to spend time alone in our rooms. I didn't have a roommate—one in human form that is, but that voice, that reassuring voice was with me.

The only tool I had to pass the time was my Bible. I tried to hyper-focus in an attempt to retain the words on the pages because the medications kept my brain in a cloudy fog. My eyes would strain with blurry vision and well with tears, but it was a hurdle I just couldn't conquer. I couldn't even read the words on the page.

I'd always derived comfort from those words and yet I couldn't get past the effects of the drugs. So I shut the Bible and held it to my chest. Closing my eyes, I heard the voice again. The voice read the scriptures to me and this time, my mind retained everything that I heard.

In grade school, I had attempted to read the Bible many times. I spent many hours memorizing verses for my confirmation and growth in the church. This time when the voice read to me, I was able to see those words and appreciate and understand them in a whole new way—from the Light who created me.

He reminded me to be quiet and listen to His words, and as I did I was filled up with unconditional love. It was the only thing that sustained me. I felt complete peace. By the time God finished with a lesson for me, I would have the clear understanding about what was next. I worked for God and I would remind myself of that before I'd walk out of my room to participate in yet another group therapy session.

When we were alone in the group without the staff, I would tell the other patients stories to give them hope. God filled me with downloads for each of them. I could see how lost they all were. They had changed and their lights within were being extinguished. They had given up.

We were a little family. I worked with each and every one of those people for hours and hours for the several days I was held captive. As I scanned the room with my eyes, in my thoughts I cried out to my Creator. *My God, they are lost. Like the sheep in a flock that has drifted far from the field, they cannot find their Master and they don't know what to do. They have forgotten who they were and they are completely vulnerable.*

There was such negativity and despair in the hospital. On the few occasions when they allowed me to go outside, I felt such relief. I could be close to God outside in the fresh air. I could see the bridge between Heaven and earth. I had learned to see it with my heart.

Even in this horrible place, even under the influence of all those medications, the connection with God could not be extinguished. It grew stronger each day. There was no doubt in my mind that the bridge was made strong through my connection to the one who created me.

Smokers were allowed outside several times a day for a smoke break. If you didn't smoke, you were only allowed half the time the smokers were allowed outside. So I took up smoking to spend time outside with God.

I helped patients all day long and quietly cried at night alone in my bed until the drugs they gave me forced me to fall asleep. I desperately missed my family. My children were only three and six and I knew they didn't understand where their mother had gone. It must have been confusing and frightening for them disappearing suddenly from their lives. But I had no choice. I was stuck there for the duration.

So I focused on the job I had promised God I would do. *I was the rock. I was the light.* I did exactly what God had taught me in Heaven. I realized the rock simply meant for me to be a vehicle for God to use. I let go and let Him work through me and as I did my light would shine.

## Paul

My fellow patients would say, "Erica, I think you are an angel." I think they were seeing my light, God's light. It happened frequently and I didn't think much of it until one day when I was attending a therapy session with the group.

We were painting small wooden birdhouses when an elderly man walked in, shuffled over and sat down next to me. There were no introductions. In fact, the rest of the room didn't seem to notice him. I turned to say hello and I looked into his eyes.

God began to download information to me as He has since the moment I returned from my NDE. I could see into this man's heart. He was a cattle rancher from out west. At one time, he had a very successful ranching business that brought him a great deal of wealth, but he had lost all of his money though gambling and drinking excessively. He'd made several bad choices during his life. Most of those choices had been made in his best interest and at the expense of others, including his family.

He was broken. He was empty. His light was extinguished. He'd even tried to commit suicide. His family had him committed in a desperate attempt to save him.

"Paul," I said.

"You know me?" he asked.

"Well, not technically. God knows you and I work for Him," I added. The color drained from his tanned leathered face. "You look like you've seen a ghost." His eyes welled and tears rolled down his face. With a shaking hand, he reached to pull a Kleenex from the box on the table.

"I know you speak the truth," he said. "My family brought me all this way so I could get help. I didn't want help; I wanted to die. I'm embarrassed and ashamed of what I've done to my family and I don't even know who I have become. I have so much guilt. I wouldn't even talk to my family. I just sat there silent the entire trip.

"I'm not a praying man, but I was so desperate that I found myself asking God, if there even was a God, to help me if I had to live. I couldn't risk looking more helpless than I already did to my family so I didn't say these things aloud, I just thought them. I must be crazy because I heard a voice. This voice was not my own and it was not from anyone in the car. No one else could hear this voice. They were busy doing other things. This voice sounded so familiar. It said, 'Paul, I love you. I'm sending someone to help you. She works for me.'"

After a moment, Paul continued. "I was in shock that I got a response to my request, but somehow I managed to instantly follow it with a question. 'God, if this is really you and you are real, make this person an angel so that I have no doubt that this is real and that you're hearing me. If you do that I'll be willing to let you help me.' I told myself that this would be next to impossible, so if it did happen, which I strongly doubted, I would have no choice, but to believe it. That was the end of the conversation."

Paul added, "After several more hours in the car I arrived here. My family admitted me and left. I had long forgotten about that conversation in the car. I forgot about that voice. So here I am. I walked in this door and I heard that darn voice again.

"*Go sit,*' said the voice. There was this blaring light in the room. I hadn't seen a light like this before. It didn't hurt my eyes, but I was drawn to it. Without hesitation, my feet walked right over to it and something sat me in this chair. Then I heard that voice again.

"*Look,*' said the voice. So I looked into the light and I saw you." Paul softly whimpered like a small child. "I knew who you were," he said. "I haven't seen a ghost. I've seen an angel."

I took his hand in mine and held it. "God is real," I said.

"Indeed. He is real and He loves me," said Paul.

# ERICA MCKENZIE

At this point, Paul was crying and our conversation drew attention from the rest of the people in the room. Some of the patients came close and one of them said to Paul, "Oh, I see you've met our Angel. Welcome."

A childlike smile grew on Paul's face and I could see the peace of God flow through him and into his heart. That man was changed, yet I did not do it. God did.

I spent several hours with Paul sharing my lessons from Planet Heaven, my earthly experiences, and encouraged him to grow the gift of being quiet and listening to the voice within. By now, I was quite good at it because I had been doing it my entire life. He learned what happened to me when I chose to stifle the voice of God. Teaching him to see that God was love and how the very connection to God grew the love that would make him strong was an important lesson for Paul. It was the power he needed in his life to find the joy and healing he was seeking. He learned that fear was the opposite of love.

By choosing love, there would be no room for fear. I explained all the things attached to fear so he could recognize them. He heard the lessons I had learned from the edge of hell and my earthly lessons about that fear prior to my death. I told him it was important to learn these things because he could use that knowledge on his earthly journey.

"If you allow it, Paul, this knowledge will become your power; the kind of power that will help you become an advocate for yourself. This means you'll be able to make better choices. Keep listening to that voice within. You're learning to discern when it is the voice of God or of ego. Have patience and learn to love yourself. This connection to the voice of Spirit will help you do so. The more you're open to receiving this love, the more you'll be able to go on and receive the love your family has been trying to give you. Then you'll be able to do

122

something you've been unable to do for a long time—give love back to them. It's a beautiful thing. It's easy. All you have to do is be quiet and listen."

We spent several more days together and during that time, I witnessed something wonderful. I witnessed Paul rediscover his value. He was so thankful that his attempt to take his life weeks prior had been unsuccessful. What once was lost was now found.

We identified his gifts and the tangible tools that would help him to grow these gifts. We then discussed how to use the gifts. I explained to him how I had learned that these God-given gifts are our uniqueness.

"This is important, Paul, so pay close attention," I said. "Your uniqueness is your value and your value becomes your contribution here on this earthly journey." If we don't value ourselves, the very person God made, we risk stifling His voice. It took me dying to realize how I had it all wrong. We may come from different backgrounds and have gone through different struggles, obstacles and tragedies, but we both chose to stifle God's voice and in doing so, we became lost.

"God gave me the chance to come back and get it right this time. It's never too late to start valuing who you are. God will help you because he loves you. You're worth it, Paul. We are all worth it. With God, all things are possible. I have seen it in Heaven and now I continue to see it here on earth. There's a bridge right in front of us between Heaven and earth. I'll help you learn how to grow that bridge and make the connection if you like."

I adopted Paul while at the hospital. He was like a little child, excited, joy-filled and renewed. I sat back and smiled for the first time in that place as I reflected on my experience with him. Next to holding my children, there was nothing better than witnessing another human recognizing something they had come into this world with but had long forgotten— *their value!*

Helping people was the only way I could keep myself from going crazy. I was a messenger of God for them. That's who I am and that's what I do. Helping them helped save me.

These people really thought that God didn't love them, but He did. They believed what the doctors and other people had told them—that they were crazy and didn't really hear God's voice. They had lost hope.

I shared my story, where I had gone, and the messages God had given me. I showed them that God loves them in order to help them learn to embrace their uniqueness and love themselves. I taught them how to make a connection with God. I said that God could help guide their life instead of letting people influence them and make them feel worthless and horrible.

However, despite this Divine guidance, I still had to contend with the hospital staff. It didn't take long for me to figure out how to work the system. If I talked about God to the hospital staff, they'd increase my meds, and when I denied God they lowered them. At one point, they medicated me with eleven different drugs.

To get my med levels down enough so I could actually function required me to deny my connection to God and my trip to Heaven. I realized I was learning how to be quiet and listen to God's voice in the midst of a stressful and challenging time. There was a time to be silent and there was a time to speak. It didn't matter if I gave the staff all the right answers; the staff still tried hard to test me and trip me up.

"Did God give you special messages, Mrs. McKenzie?"

"No. He didn't give me special messages."

"Did you go to Heaven, Mrs. McKenzie?"

"No. I did not go to Heaven."

They drilled me every way they could. I denied my special connection to God repeatedly, when all I wanted to do was shout to the world, *"God lives! Heaven is for real and Love is the answer!"*

They continued to watch me closely. Often they would enter my room at night to tell me to shut off my light and go to bed only to find when they opened the door there was no light left on. I was sound asleep.

They would interrogate me the next day.

"There was a light coming from your room. You were supposed to be asleep. When we opened the door, your light would shut off. What were you doing?"

They knew it wasn't physically possible for me to get up, turn off the only light switch in my room, and jump back into bed prior to them opening the door.

That evening a nurse entered my room. "Are you hiding a light somewhere?" She asked. "You're not allowed to have a flashlight, a lighter, or whatever you are using to create that light."

What the heck was she talking about? "I have no light," I said sleepily.

Unsatisfied with my response, she turned my room light on and forced me to stand with my arms raised from my sides. She patted me down and then searched the room and through the few personal things I was allowed to keep. Nothing. She found nothing.

"Ugh!" Frustrated, she finally gave and up shut my light off. "Lights out!" she commanded and left.

*You've got to be kidding me*, I thought. Now I'm getting labeled as the troublemaker and I didn't even do anything. I had no idea what light they were talking about. I didn't have any lights.

Then I heard the voice say to me, *"The light is of me and I am with you."*

Are you kidding me, God? Of course! With you, all things are possible. And with that, I laughed for the first time in days.

Despite what one may think, God has a great sense of humor and He was good at cheering me up. I had promised God I would work for Him. I needed to shout the messages God had given me like I needed air to breathe. Everyone deserved to know how loved they were! But he was showing me that there was a time and place to share this knowledge. There would be times to be silent and there would be times to speak. There would be times that I would feel alone, but he was always with me.

For almost a month, I watched man at his most evil self. I felt bad seeing the doctors and medical staff oppress the patients. I could see the ego driven self in action and this was a much-needed lesson for me. I needed to pay attention. It was so hard to witness because these patients were good people. I could see their hearts. They were good people who had made bad choices, some out of fear, some out of habit, others out of convenience, some out of lack of knowledge, and some simply because they were lost.

During that time, I was reminded of the deep sadness God felt as he watched the earth in flames and the souls left behind. My passion for God and my experience burned inside me like a brilliant light. To deny Him was to deny the very essence of myself. I remembered God's sadness for his children and the lesson of free will.

I had two choices while committed: I could claim a mental

breakdown or I could claim I talked with God in Heaven. I knew the only way I could secure my release from the hospital was to choose to act as if I had a mental breakdown. I was filled with peace knowing that this was what I was to do. It was what God wanted.

Had I insisted that I had gone to Heaven, I would have been operating in ego. That would have been an easy choice. But it wasn't about me; it was about what was best for me, and God's voice was best for me so I listened.

I learned to say, "I'm not having thoughts or messages from God," or "This medicine helps me feel normal." I had to do this for a period of time in order for them to trust me to continue with their programming and drugs when I returned home.

My last day on the psych ward, as messed up as it sounds, was actually one of the saddest days of my recollection. I had grown to love each of those other patients. We were a flock. Somehow through God's greatness He had managed to bring hope to that unit despite all of the obstacles we each endured.

I allowed myself to be the vehicle for God during my stay. God had given me the gift of growing the love to build a connection with Him in their hearts. I knew by the time I left, as sad as I was and as much as I would miss them, I didn't have to worry because they were ready. It was now up to each of them to choose to grow and sustain their own connection to God.

# HEALTH IN THE BODY

*"To keep the body in good health is a duty. Otherwise we shall
not be able to keep our mind strong and clear."*

Buddha

Once home, I flung my arms around my babies and gathered them to me. I didn't want to let go. I buried my face in their hair and inhaled their scent. I kissed their sweet faces delighted by the sight of them. I had missed them terribly. It had been far too long since I'd seen their beautiful smiles.

As I embraced my little ones, I finally understood the importance of the gift of unconditional love that God gives. My love was so strong for my children, and yet it couldn't touch the enormity of love I felt from God for each and every one of us.

Being away from my children was the hardest thing about being committed. I could take the drugs, and the rules, and the programming. I could even take the deep sadness I felt denying God, but nothing was worse than being kept from my children. I thanked God I was finally home with them.

When the hospital released me, part of my ongoing out-patient rehabilitation was to work with the doctors for many weeks and attend meetings with therapists. They needed to see I had made a lifestyle change. It was so difficult to lead this double life. Yet, during this time God continued to talk to me, reassuring me of His presence.

My mom stayed with me another week or so. She had taken such good care of my children and home. Once she left, Derek worked from home to make sure I was okay and following the doctor's orders. Per instruction from the doctor, I had to let Derek watch me take my medications. I would have to show him the meds that I was taking. The doctors told him to be careful that I continued to take my medicine. While I might think I was okay, I wasn't quite yet.

There were three major problems I had with taking the medications the doctor prescribed during my treatment. The first was that when sleeping, I experienced terrifying hallucinations. This affected my sleep over a period of time. As a result, I became exhausted and depressed. Second, the drugs impaired my ability to think clearly. Third and most important, taking these medications stifled my ability to communicate and connect with God.

My trip to Planet Heaven with God was real and my ability to hear God's voice and maintain a connection, a relationship with him, was as real as the relationships I had with my husband and children. They were completely different from the terrifying thoughts and hallucinations I experienced while on these medications. How ironic that the very drugs they gave me to stop my "hallucinations with "God" actually created terrifying thoughts and hallucinations of an entirely different kind.

As a nurse, I knew they were drug-induced. I had to question – were these drugs ever therapeutic for anyone? Being on them sure didn't feel as though they could be helpful to anyone. However, I am more inclined to believe that since my body didn't physiologically need them, I was having adverse effects from them instead of therapeutic effects. But shouldn't the doctors have known this would happen? Or maybe the more critical question was, knowing that my body didn't need these drugs what was I going to do? Especially since the doctors refused to consider an alternative diagnosis.

My husband was needed back at work and no one could stay home with me to monitor my every move. This gave me the opportunity to wean myself off the drugs I was forced to take. I began the detox I should have started more than a month before.

Derek put me on the honor system and trusted I was taking my meds. Instead, I flushed them down the toilet. As a nurse, I knew I had to completely clean out my system in order to begin truly healing my body. We had finally reached a point where Derek could see my progress and didn't feel the enormous stress he'd had from the day he first found me in the hospital. Eventually, I was strong and healthy enough to earn a few small privileges back. But this was just the beginning of a long road to recovery from the damage that had been done to my body

Driving presented a problem because the circulation to my hands was restricted and this caused them to go numb just holding onto the steering wheel for any length of time. When I did so, my heart started to beat erratically and my breathing would become labored. Much of the time, I wasn't able to drive because of it. This was challenging as a mother of two growing children. I didn't have family or friends that lived nearby and calling Derek was not an option. He couldn't drive them. He was needed at his work. Besides, instead of feeling like I was his wife, for the past few months, I felt more like his child, and I couldn't stand the thought of disappointing him again. I desperately missed being a wife and mother so I was determined not to lose the few privileges I had gained back due to incompetence. Hoping to improve the numbness in my hands, I felt compelled to seek the advice of a doctor. My insurance dictated that I see a general practitioner so I made the appointment.

During my visit a health assessment was performed. The assessment revealed tachycardia, a slight heart murmur, high blood pressure, and numbness in my extremities. When we were finished, I walked out of that office with a prescription for an antianxiety medication and a recommendation to see a counselor for depression, a cardiologist and neurologist. But I wasn't depressed. I just couldn't hold onto the steering wheel, I told myself. I quickly dismissed the idea of seeing another counselor. Why should I? It seemed each time I confided in one, it was clear they didn't really listen. I made appointments with the cardiologist and neurologist but their earliest availability was three months away. However, I did fill the new prescription. The next day, I knew I would have to drive the kids to school so I retrieved the medication and read the warning label on the bottle – "Warning, do not drive while taking this medication. It may impair your ability to think clearly." Seriously? I was desperate, so I decided to take half of the recommended dose. The therapeutic effect was that I lay parked on the couch for the duration of the day, unable to take the kids to school. Lesson learned.

My body was desperately trying to tell me something and it was time I listened. Up to this point, my life had been vast and chaotic, and went in directions I would never have expected. I'd always felt as though I should be able to handle it all without breaking into tiny little pieces. I wasn't fragile and I wasn't crazy, but for years I struggled to keep up with my family, work and the pressures of society. I'd been a "people pleaser" and I had blamed myself for how miserable I felt. In the process, I ignored my body's own amazing feedback systems: my feelings and intuition.

I had so many conflicting feelings, like doubt, loneliness, anger, sadness, desperation, frustration, joy, happiness, and lack of self-worth to name a few. I was a map and my feelings were all over it. I had been apologizing for, suppressing, doubting and doing everything with my feelings rather than acknowledging and embracing them.

And then there was my intuition – that's my inner voice. I knew the difference between my voice and the voice of God. They were totally different, and yet I knew that my voice would not be as strong and effective without God's voice. I saw it was very much like the relationship between the brain and the mind and I pondered on the lessons I learned in Heaven.

I had finally found the courage to start listening to my feelings, intuition and God first, using them as powerful tools and as a catalyst for creating a healthy life. This meant instead of expecting the doctors, or anyone else for that matter, to know what was best for me, it was time for me to get real with myself by taking full responsibility for my health.

A few months later Derek finally said, "I've noticed a big change in you. You've come a long way and I can see you're doing really well. I'm proud of you."

A sharp stab of guilt shot through me and I closed my eyes and swallowed hard. "Here I go," I told myself. It was time for me to mentally detox from my old way of handling my feelings.

I still had to tell him I'd been lying to him about my meds. I knew it was the only thing I could do to move forward with my healing on all levels. "My feelings, my intuition and God are my tools," I reminded myself. I heard God's voice say, *"The truth will set you free."*

So I braced myself and said, "I'm glad you agree I'm doing so well, but I need to tell you something, Derek." I prayed he'd forgive me and it wouldn't damage the trust we had begun to rebuild since my discharge. The silence stretched between us and I took a deep breath and continued. "I haven't taken the drugs for a few months."

"What? You promised me!" he blurted out. "What are you thinking?"

"Please, Derek! I really need you to listen to me. I'm *not* bipolar. It was the diet pills I was on for almost nine years. Neither you nor the doctors would listen." I reached out and squeezed his arm to reassure him. "I tried to tell you in the hospital room, but you wouldn't listen to me. What I really needed was to detox, not be committed and drugged.

"I knew I couldn't tell you my plan after I was released because of the events leading up to my hospitalization. How could that doctor treat my condition properly if he chose to disregard the chronic use of a class four narcotic designed for short-term use as the underlying cause of my illness? His judgment of me, deliberate dismissal of my addiction to the diet pills and his refusal to investigate my claim put me at risk. I know you thought he knew what was best for me and you were only trying to help because you love me. But since no one would listen, I *had* to take responsibility and help myself."

I forced myself to breathe. "And I did it! I totally did it! I got off the drugs." Speaking to my husband, I embraced my feelings, my intuition and God's voice. I advocated for myself! I felt empowered and awakened.

He was silent for a moment before he answered. Derek, the thinker. I could tell by his furrowed brow that he was really weighing what I had just told him. He exhaled slowly. "I'm so sorry I let the doctor convince me to allow them to put you in there. I didn't know. I thought I was doing what was best for you. Seeing you in that condition, I was convinced the doctor knew best."

I could feel his regret, along with his confusion and frustration during the past few months. I looked up at him. "It's okay. It's not your fault. I'm not blaming you, myself, Dr. Imanass, Dr. Enabler or anyone else. I forgive myself, I forgive you and the doctors because of the things I learned in Heaven. That day when I finally found my voice and the first thing out of my mouth was all about my journey to Heaven with God was because I couldn't contain myself, Derek. There are no words to explain how incredible it was to be there.

"God wanted to give Dr. Imanass the opportunity to reconnect with Him and I was to be the vehicle for it but when I tried to tell the doctor about my trip to Heaven with God, he chose ego. God not only wanted to give the doctor this opportunity but he also needed me to experience the state of our healthcare system through the lesson of having been committed. It prepared me to see firsthand how broken the system is and how that affects the patients so I could help change the health care protocol and support the people, teaching them to become self-advocates. I know that God planned it that way."

Derek stood quietly as I continued to explain it to him and it poured out so fast. Going through the experience in the hospital revealed to me a lot about myself. I genuinely had no idea I would be able to view this tragic experience as a great opportunity for learning but honestly, it's true. I am thankful for all of the experiences in the facility because these lessons have shown me how strong a person I really am. It's true that no one can define my potential greatness. But I don't have to be a victim, and that is empowering! At the same time, I knew before I could begin to fix the system and help others, I had to heal myself. I was broken, so it was going to be hard work because it was a constant battle between healing and changing me. I understood these to be two completely different approaches, and according to everything I had just learned in Heaven, it was more evident to me than ever that the answer wasn't to change me. Even if the staff had the best intentions for restoring my health, it was clear that their approach was going to lead to changing, not healing, me. I identified the need for education once more, but this time it was essential for all of us, as I came to comprehend the significant meaning of the word "change." I understood for many that the word change had taken on a meaning that had the potential to improve or destroy the human condition.

And yet there was no doubt in my mind that all the obstacles I had been through and the roadblocks that were ahead were no match for the knowledge I gained in Heaven. I knew that with God all things were possible.

I continued to share my feelings with Derek. I've spent my entire life trying to be everything to everyone and in the process I lost myself. I have loved all of you, but I couldn't love myself. I didn't think I was good enough or deserving of that self-love. And I felt selfish for wanting it. Now I see that way of thinking was not healthy because thinking that way and doing those things changed me and led me in the opposite direction from becoming a self-advocate and completing my earthly mission.

My NDE has not changed my life. It has given me life by opening my eyes with those glasses to see my value. It has reawakened me to the real Erica, the little child who was in touch with God and His gifts before I let fear in and started to stifle my feelings, doubted my intuition and drowned out the voice of God in an effort to listen to everyone Listening to my feelings, intuition and God first, I found that I could use them as powerful tools and as a catalyst for creating a healthy life. I knew what was best for me. Which meant I could finally begin to fully access my blueprint. It was time for me to get real with myself by taking full responsibility for my health. So with the support of God, Derek, and my family, armed with my tools, I began the long and challenging road that would lead to healing, valuing my life, and becoming an advocate for myself and others. My hope is not just to have the strength to change but to also be the change needed to bring light to the world.

# HEALTH IN THE MIND

*"You will find as you look back upon your life that the moments
when you have really lived, are the moments when you have
done things in the spirit of love."*

Henry Drummond

Over the course of the next few months, I continued to
become stronger. Each day my mental clarity
sharpened, I felt better, and it became much easier for
me to hear God's voice. Then one afternoon, I received an
interesting download urging me to call my Uncle John. He was
the uncle that I had called years ago to tell him his father had a
heart attack and he was going to die. I told him at that time to
leave everything and go at once, making the four-hour drive to
see his father, before he crossed. I knew that he would listen and
I'm glad he did because he was able to say goodbye.

Uncle John had heard about my health and my being
committed to the psych ward from my parents. I think since
the day I gave him the message about grandpa he knew that I
had a special gift.

I was a bit hesitant to make the call since I had not been
home that long. What would he think of me? But *"I work for
God and there is no fear when God is there."* "Feelings,
intuition and God," I reminded myself. So I made the call.

"How are you feeling?" Uncle John asked.

"I'm feeling much better, thank you."

"I'm glad to hear it. Please take care of yourself."

I could feel the sincerity behind his words and it meant a lot to me. While talking with Uncle John, I recalled something that happened in the emergency room with the three angel nurses. I had not remembered it until that moment.

There was a brief second in the emergency room, after the three angel nurses spoke to me, when I felt compelled to look to my left at the partitioned curtain. I could see someone standing behind it. At first, I could only see a man's shiny black dress shoes, and then his black dress pants. My gaze moved upward to reveal a man. It was my Uncle John, dressed in a business suit.

He looked at me with admiration and at the same time, he looked past me. I knew he wasn't dead. But I wondered how it was possible that he could be standing here with me? He lived several hours away in Omaha, Nebraska.

I was downloaded with the message that he would be the next person in my family to die and cross over to Heaven. It wasn't going to be right away, but he would have no more than the digits on his feet of years left on earth. God was giving him a glimpse into the afterlife and I was the connector.

I felt sick at the thought of knowing this information. How could I possibly tell anyone in my family about this experience, especially after everything they had just experienced with me? They'd send me back to the psych ward.

Why had I been allowed to see this? What was I supposed to do with this information besides grow an ulcer from the knowledge, worrying about my Uncle John?

What did *digits on his feet* mean and why didn't I just hear a number? I knew there were ten digits total, five on each foot. Under my breath, I said to God, "I don't know what I am to do with this information you gave me, but I know I made a promise to work for you. I just didn't think it was going to be this hard. Please help me to have patience with myself, I know it is a gift and Please God, give me the words that you want me to say to him."

The next thing I knew out came the words just as they had in the hospital room with the doctor.

"Uncle John, do you remember when I called to tell you grandpa was going to die? I said you needed to immediately make the four hour drive to the hospital to see your father before he passed?"

"I do," he said.

"Do you remember I said that God told me?"

"Yes."

"Well, I have another message for you from God. But I need to know it will be safe to tell you because when I mentioned God during my hospital stay, I was admitted to the psych ward."

"I promise it is safe to tell me," he answered.

Undeterred by the uncertainty I felt for my safety, I was determined that fear would no longer be a part of my life. I let go and let God worry about the rest as I took a deep breath and told him the entire story of my trip to Heaven. I shared the lessons I learned with God, what I saw, and how wonderful it was to be in Heaven. Heaven was our true home. There was no pain, just love.

I told him I didn't want to come back, not even for my children. That is how wonderful it was there. I also described seeing him in the emergency room and shared how much God loved him. I mentioned that I was glad that he moved back to be close to his family and encouraged him to enjoy every moment with them. Someday he would get a new mission from

God because he was a great teacher and a much-needed leader. His earth life was preparing him for an important role and unlike me, his new assignment would be in Heaven.

There was silence on the other end of the phone and my heart starting pounding. I thought to myself *My God, what did I just do? I shouldn't have told him.*

I didn't mention anything about him only having ten years left. I just couldn't wrap my head around how to tell him. What if I was wrong? I would have to live with the guilt of making him feel needless worry and suffering for the rest of my life.

But what if I was right? And knowing this information could assist him in some way? I felt light-headed and a bead of sweat fell from my brow. I couldn't afford to make the wrong choice. Besides I wasn't even qualified to make this choice. As these thoughts raced through my mind, I felt myself moving towards my ego and that was a place I didn't care to be.

"Help me God, I don't know what you want me to say. Please give me discernment and give me peace." I had all but forgotten that Uncle John was still on the phone when I heard sniffling followed by a cracking in his voice as he spoke, "Thank you for sharing that with me. I needed to hear it. God is great," he said.

At once the sensation of peace entered into me. "Yes, He is," I answered.

He didn't ask me if I knew how much time he had. It didn't matter to him. I could tell from visiting with him that his heart was ready to leave this earthly journey at any time. It was then I had accepted that there was no need to mention ten years.

For almost a decade, which included several sleepless nights, I was at a loss to understand how knowing this information could be helpful to anyone. My uncle died on Friday, January 14, 2011.

When I heard the news I remembered what the voice had said, but realized it had only been nine years, not ten. Why didn't God tell me the truth?

At once, I heard the voice say, *"He would have no more than the digits on his feet in years left on this earth."*

My head was spinning and I had to sit down. How could I have forgotten? Many years before, at the young age of sixteen, my uncle lost his toe in a lawn mower accident. The fact was my uncle only had nine toes or digits! God was telling the truth! It had been nine years since I received that message.

God told me my uncle had nine years left to help me validate that when I was quiet and listened, I would receive knowledge from the other side of the veil that could help me and help others on our earthly journey. I realized that we all have these same opportunities to be quiet and listen and to receive information to help us on our own journeys.

I will never really know what sharing that message with my uncle meant for him personally, as it was not for me to know. It was just my job to plant the seed I'd been given and by doing so God gave me a gift; a valuable lesson in discernment.

## *The Gift of Service*

God gave me a clear download after I returned from my NDE, to work with Hospice patients. And so, I became a hospice nurse case manager. There were two reasons for this. First, He wanted me to help them shift their perception of death and the fear surrounding it through my knowledge of the afterlife and my experiences. Second, He wanted me to be able to see that giving of my time and love to others left less time to focus on the problems I was having.

I'd become depressed at times by the frustration of dealing with my on-going physical health issues. But, when I actively focused on being of service to someone who was less fortunate than I, the most incredible thing happened – I didn't feel depressed about anything. In fact, quite the opposite. I was filled with gratitude and appreciated everything I had including my health challenges. These experiences really humbled me and shifted my perception of how I viewed the current challenges I was facing.

Through it, I became conscious of the truth, this time on a deeper level; God wasn't going to give me more than I could handle. Giving to others quickly became a tool that generated healing and balance in my life. It was the Rippling Effect again and I was seeing it all unfold.

I loved my job but throughout my training, I was taught not to counsel the patients and remain neutral when approached by the patient or family about crossing over. They taught me to deflect those questions to the assigned clergy or social worker. However, something didn't seem right. A rule follower by nature, I was still a part of that generation that grew up respecting their elders and instilled with fear not to question authority. I wasn't being disrespectful intentionally. I just had questions. I had an incredible experience and an assignment attached to it. I was not questioning the credentials of the clergy or social workers. It wasn't about that. I was questioning the clarity of their reasoning not to make this information available to these dying people.

I kept thinking, *but I've been there*. What if the roles were reversed? What if I were the one dying? Who would I really want to talk to about what happens when we die? As helpful as others were trying to be, I just couldn't let go of this knowledge and wisdom that I had obtained and knew it would bring relief to those facing death. *I've died! I've been to Heaven and back!* Wouldn't I want to hear from someone like me? I was a near-death experiencer so of course it just made sense. I knew I could help eliminate their fears if given the chance.

You can probably guess that I took advantage of every opportunity I was given to share my knowledge and help ease the fears of dying patients. I didn't plan to tell them or worry if I didn't. I simply found the courage to let go of my fear and ego, step aside, and let God work through me. My intention was never to receive anything back from these people who were so close to death's door. I was there to serve them in their time of need. But you must know, by doing so, the most wonderful thing happened. Each time, I was given an incredible gift of love!

Here I was being welcomed with open arms into these people's lives in what was to be their final, most intimate moments on earth. I didn't have one bad experience. I was welcomed with love and such thankful hearts by these people. I couldn't believe it. This gift of love was instrumental in my healing.

With each patient came new experiences. It was always different and different was beautiful. Each time I willingly did the work God had for me, I learned, and through this knowledge, I grew stronger in my body, mind and spirit. That strength transformed into a powerful method of healing for my body.

Also, with each patient I worked with, I made sure I was quiet and listened. First to the patient, then to Spirit and finally I would speak when and if I was told as I shared the message I was given. There were times I asked them what they were seeing, hearing or feeling throughout their journey and if they felt compelled to share. When they shared what they were experiencing, it opened the door for me to share my knowledge and wisdom from Heaven. Other times, I was given a download for the patient. The download was specific for that person and would serve to shift their perception of the death experience. There were also times when my job was to be quiet and listen as no words were needed. Through these lessons, they received a gift from their creator.

## Snowflake

One particular story comes to mind. I had a patient called Betty. She had such a heart for animals. I developed an instant bond with her as we each shared a heart for God's creatures. Betty had a little dog that never left her side. That dog remained in that hospital bed snuggled next to her 24/7. It was her faithful companion.

She told me that she also used to have a beautiful white cat, but like Betty, it got cancer. She said her cat had passed a few months ago. A few days prior to Betty's death, I made my scheduled nurse visit to her house. My heart was heavy for her husband, who would be left behind. I rather enjoyed our visits. She was in such pain yet she managed to find moments of laughter despite being completely bed-ridden and weak.

I sat down on her bed. She looked at me with a familiar smile but today I saw through her smile and into her heart. I knew it was to be the last time I would see her in her earthly body.

"Betty, I'm going to miss you so much. I'm happy for you because it is so wonderful in Heaven. Remember, I told you I didn't want to come back, not even for my children."

"Yes, you argued with God. Who does that?" she added. There was silence followed by laughter. "I'm glad God has a sense of humor," she said. "I think that's what's making it so easy for me to let go and go home. I'm ready but Paul is not. Would you help him with that Erica?"

Paul was her husband. I suggested we pray together and both ask God for help with that. I took her hands in mine. They were bone and sore, riddled, thin flesh. I gently held them and said, "God, Betty is ready to come home to be with you in that wonderful place called Heaven. Please help Paul to have peace with understanding that it is time for Betty to be with you. Help him to somehow begin to see the bridge that exists between Heaven and earth." No sooner did we finish that prayer than Paul came home from running errands.

They were the loveliest elderly couple. They had been together for a very long time. He only left her side when a hospice staff member would come for a visit. Paul came in and had a seat next to us. We began to make small talk, when suddenly Betty's eyes were abruptly drawn to something on the opposite side of the room.

She gasped and pointed with purpose, "My cat! It's Snowflake! Can you see her? Here, kitty, kitty!"

Paul and I looked and at first, we saw nothing. And then the dog began to bark and jumped from the bed as if he were going to chase something. It was then we saw it. We all saw it. The cat came from behind the television and ran from the dog taking refuge behind the recliner. Well, there was only one of us in that room on morphine so we knew that we weren't all hallucinating.

We all saw Betty's cat that had already crossed over! God had sent a sign for Paul. It was the appearance of Snowflake the white cat.

"Hurry, Paul! Go get Snowflake!" shouted Betty. "Here, kitty, kitty," she kept calling for her.

Paul quickly let the dog outside and scurried to the recliner. He looked behind it and under it, but Snowflake was not to be found. I took this opportunity to teach Paul about after-death communication and helped him to see that not only does life continue on, but crossing to the other side of the veil doesn't mean we have to cease communication with our loved ones. Rather, if we can shift our perception of death, we come to understand that our loved ones never leave us. We can communicate and experience an unbreakable connection with them on the other side!

"It's similar to talking with God." I said. "Many times we find ourselves talking to our Creator and we feel He doesn't listen, he doesn't hear our pleas, but this is not true. He does. We must be quiet and listen because He always answers us. It is the same with our loved ones. "Paul," I said, "The most important thing is to believe. When we choose to believe in something greater than ourselves, we can open our heart and learn a beautiful, exciting new way of continuing our relationships with those we love. Believe and you will see Heaven all around you. It is then that you will come to know the bridge between Heaven and earth is made by your heart."

## *The Dove*

I had figured out how to keep this bridge of after-death communication open. Sure enough, each time my request was fulfilled. Knowing their death wasn't a goodbye forever, I asked my Hospice patients to visit me after they crossed over, just to say "hello." It was remarkable to have an opportunity to experience them following through with a request that was agreed upon prior to their crossing. These experiences came in all sorts of ways. Many times animals played a starring role.

One Sunday afternoon I was on call. The on-call shift required me to make an unscheduled visit to any patient who would call the hospice center requesting one. It was a twelve-hour shift and generally easy money. I would get paid regardless of whether or not I received a call. Personally, I dreaded taking the on-call shift. While I loved helping people, I never knew what situation I would walk into when I received a call and it always caused me a bit of anxiety.

Don't get me wrong, I felt confident with my assessment skills as a nurse. My anxiety stemmed from the question I often asked myself when taking a call, *Would I be able to serve my patients, providing the loving care they deserved as a nurse messenger?*

But God always has a plan and this time, Ms. Marge was her name. She was a loving, heavyset elderly woman and such a delight. She was a bird watcher. White doves were her favorite. Kansas isn't known for their white doves, but nonetheless she loved them so. In her younger years, she dedicated a significant amount of vacation time traveling to spectacular places with the hope of stealing a glance at those birds. Every time I would make my way to her house for her nurse visit, the conversation was same.

"Good afternoon, Ms. Marge. How are you feeling today?"

"I am feeling like the white dove," she'd say. "I can't wait until I can fly away."

She would think of the white dove flying to magical places to help pass the time, and I sensed it brought her some solace from the pain of the rectal cancer that had spread throughout her body. She was a tough woman, but I could sense her pain from the grimaces on her face when she didn't think I was looking.

My time was spent listening to her stories about her life and of the happier times she'd had. I think she had some type of bird in practically every story she told.

She never blamed God for her failing health. In fact, the last time I saw Ms. Marge she asked me to tell her about Heaven again.

"Dear, I'm tired. I just want to spread my wings and fly like the white dove. Can you ask God if He wouldn't mind helping me to fly? What do you think, dear? Will God do that for me? He talks to you. Will you ask Him for me? Go on now. Ask God to help me. I am too weak." she said.

I took her frail hand and smiled as I looked into her beautiful blue eyes. I said, "God has heard you, Ms. Marge and the answer is yes." Her eyes welled with tears but not of sorrow. They were tears of joy and relief. She gave me the most loving smile back; a smile I will never forget.

As I finished my health assessment, I chose to stay and write up my report at her bedside. I wanted to spend a little more time in her presence as I had the *knowing* that the next time I would see Ms. Marge it would be in her spirit form.

"Ms. Marge, if it's not too much trouble, could you find a way to come to visit me once you cross over? It would mean so much to me."

"Of course, dear, we have already made plans."

"Plans?" I asked.

"Why yes, God talks to me too and He tells me I will come to visit you."

"How will I know it's you?" I asked.

"I shall come as a white dove and when I come you shall know it is me." Her voice was suddenly childlike as if something had come over Ms. Marge.

Of course, I thought. A white dove.

It wasn't more than a day or so later that Ms. Marge passed away.

On the third day, following that visit to Ms. Marge, a very interesting visitor made its way to the McKenzie house. It had already been an unusual day, filled with rain, and it was close to 6 pm when the storm finally broke. It was time for dinner. Normally I would give a shout-out to the kids to come downstairs for dinner, but today something made me walk up the stairs and into my eldest son's room instead. "Keenan, it's time for dinner," I said.

At once, I was compelled to look out the window from across the room. The sun had managed to peek through the clouds, leaving behind the most magical rainbow. The rainbow appeared closer to the house than I had ever remembered seeing one before.

"Keenan, look at the rainbow," I said.

Just then, I was drawn across his room and stood in front of the large window.

"*Look*," said the voice.

I glanced down outside the window to my right and nearly fell backwards in astonishment. There on our roof, a foot to the right of Keenan's window, sat a white dove just staring at me.

"Ms. Marge!" I cried. There wasn't a doubt in my mind it was our Ms. Marge. She had fulfilled her promise to come back to visit me. She said God had given her the message that she would come as a white dove.

"Come quick!" I called for my family to behold this wondrous sight. I wanted to share this moment with them. It was a learning opportunity and I wanted each of them to see her before she would decide it was time to fly away. One by one, each of my family entered the room and came to see the dove.

I regaled them all with the story of my hospice patient, Ms. Marge. I shared with them the promise that God made to send her in the spirit form as a white dove. She had come not only to fulfill that promise, but also to say goodbye and thank me for touching her life.

The rainbow quickly came and went and with it the sun. A new set of storm clouds quickly moved in, this time producing torrential rains with high winds. I was worried as Ms. Marge continued to sit on my roof unsheltered from the storm. She had not moved one inch from her spot. I cranked open the window slightly so that she could hear my voice.

"Ms. Marge, thank you so much for coming to see me. I love you. It's O.K. You can go now. Please fly, just like you said you wanted to do for so long. If you stay, I'm afraid you'll get harmed in this storm." I hesitated, wishing somehow she would come inside, but I had to shut the window. I didn't have a choice at this point because the rain was coming into the bedroom. I waited and watched as she sat there unaffected by the storm.

Being the animal lover I was, Ms. Marge or not, I could no longer bear to watch. It hurt me too much. I wanted to rescue her. I told myself I would go straighten up the kitchen from dinner and then I'd come back to check on her.

While I was cleaning the kitchen I became distracted by my children and roped into playing a game, then completing a project, coloring a picture and finally topping the evening off with two baths for my kids, a dog bath and one final load of laundry. I was exhausted, once again, by the nightly routine of motherhood.

As I made my way upstairs to do the final tuck in for the night, I stopped to kiss my daughter goodnight before making my way to my son's room.

"Mom," he said. "The white dove is still sitting outside my window. *Ms. Marge*, I thought. I quickly made my way to the window to see. Sure enough, there she was sitting in the same spot. It was still storming fairly hard and my heart sunk. How would she survive?

I didn't want to risk making my son any more upset than he already was at the sight of her, so I suggested that I stay with him to keep watch. I'd make sure she stayed safe so he could fall asleep.

When Keenan drifted off, I whispered to Ms. Marge, "Thank you for coming to visit me and you are welcome to stay as long as you wish. I trust that God will protect you and you will remain unharmed. I love you. Good night."

I was reluctant to leave her out there as I turned and walked to my room. I love animals so much it didn't seem right to leave her there, but I had no way to bring her safely inside. I just prayed that she would be safe.

Ms. Marge stayed with us in that very spot for seven days. Over the course of those days, I would set out a fresh bowl of water and seed to keep her comfortable. I invited the neighbors to come see her, too. I was so thankful for this experience and that my family and neighbors could share in this gift of love from God and Ms. Marge.

Once again, I found myself sitting at the windowsill, visiting with Ms. Marge with what had become our routine. But today's visit with Ms. Marge would be different. On the morning of the seventh day, I came to understand what the white dove symbolized. I now understood that her spirit was able to travel to and from Heaven and the transition between one state of being and another was effortless.

I smiled at the dove but addressed Ms. Marge. "I remember during hospice you talked about the white dove in many of your stories. It was your favorite bird for so long. You also mentioned God gave you the message that you would come to me as a white dove. I can't begin to tell you how much your visit has meant to me."

How was it possible she found me? As I gazed off past the roofline toward the large pine trees in our yard, in a moment of reflection on this little miracle, it came to me. "*Remember, my dear, with God all things are possible,*" Ms. Marge had said before she died.

With that, the white dove looked into my eyes just before she turned her head and flew away. I was never to see Ms. Marge again. My mind drifted to the time I spent in Heaven when God revealed to me we were eternal beings and once we left this earth our journeys would continue. From time to time, I still sense her presence. I will never forget Ms. Marge and our after death communication experience. She had given me a gift which I will always keep with me in my heart.

# THE ADVOCATE

*"Experience is not what happens to you; it's what you do with what happens to you."*

Aldous Huxley

lso following my near-death experience, I continued to exhibit a multitude of health problems that became more frequent and severe. I experienced heart and lung issues, and circulation issues that involved several visits to the emergency room with episodes of acute vaso-vagal syncope. I had a thyroid disorder, hormonal imbalances, memory loss, hot flashes, insomnia, tachycardia, panic and anxiety attacks, Reynaud's disease, circulation issues and a tonsillectomy. I underwent a total hysterectomy to treat my endometriosis, which led to surgically induced menopause. The endometriosis had spread to other organs in my body, affecting other areas such as my bladder, colon and low back. I had basal cell skin cancer that required reconstructive facial plastic surgery.

After years of struggling with health problems, I was at the end of my rope. I had consulted with general practitioners, cardiologists, neurologists, endocrinologists, psychologists, gynecologists, hematologists, urologists gastroenterologists, dermatologists, internal medicine experts, osteopathic medicine experts, physical therapists, hormone specialists, acupuncturist and even a chiropractor.

Many doctors tried but were unsuccessful in helping me to get healthy. I am forever grateful to each of them, because I feel the majority of them were doing their best with the knowledge they had access to. But something inside told me to be quiet and listen to my body. I had been to Heaven and been given an assignment. In my heart I knew nothing was going to stop me from completing it, yet I was not in any physical condition to be able to carry out this mission for God.

I was diagnosed with everything from a slight heart abnormality, possible early onset of multiple sclerosis, fibromyalgia, given additional anti-anxiety prescriptions and offered more anti-depressants. This time, my response was, *No way! Are you kidding me?* After everything I had been through there was absolutely no doubt that these medications were not the answer for my body. In fact, my intuition told me if I started taking these prescriptions, I would quickly find myself back to square one or worse because this time I had *the wisdom* to know. I felt like I had arrived at a dead end road.

I was even told on multiple occasions from different physicians that because of my lack of hormones due to the total hysterectomy, I should expect the way I felt to become my "new normal." After all, I was getting older and with age came certain "challenges." When I sought out qualified healthcare providers who were hormone specialists, I discovered their qualifications and titles varied greatly. I was given hormones via patches, creams and pellets to name a few. With each treatment, my health declined. I would stay with the "hormone specialist" for as long as I could. After all, each reassured me that this type of therapy took time to see therapeutic results.

In total, I had been under the care of six different hormone specialists. I gave them each time and only moved on when I could no longer take the undesired side effects from the latest treatments. I began to question the methods of testing because their recommendations, treatment modalities and hormone concoctions were as individual as they were. I wish I could say that all of them performed diagnostic testing but that wasn't the case. There was, however, a common link they all appeared to demonstrate regardless of doing testing or not; their lack of knowledge and understanding as to how the hormones actually worked within the body was clearly evident. This lack of knowledge was reflected in their choice of treatment modalities including prescribing and combining the hormones.

Now, I felt like a human guinea pig who had arrived at a dead end road. I wasn't interested in being an experiment or being told they had never seen a case like mine before. I was too young for full-fledged menopause. Women my age were still having babies. I felt like I was losing my mind and my body was falling apart. I continued pursuing my research, this time driven by my refusal to accept that the only answer was for me to adapt to this "new normal," and that there was nothing else that could be done to help me. But what about my blueprint and what was normal for me?

What Is Normal?! *"Do the work,"* God said. And with his instruction, this time it was unquestionable what the work meant: research. Instead of going to the pharmacy to fill more prescriptions, I went home and began to read all of the articles, the journals, books, watched videos, and listened to seminars, all the things I could get my hands on. The more research I did the stronger the confirmation that my feelings and intuition were accurate.

New Normal? Are you kidding me? I wasn't even able to recall the old normal, and honestly at this point, the more research I did, the more I began to seriously look at the strong possibility that the term *normal* might be one of the most misguided, loosely used, out of date, problematic terms in our entire society! My dictionary was within reaching distance so I grabbed it and flipped through the pages searching for the definition of normal: "Normal, conforming to the standard or the common type; usual; not abnormal; regular; natural, free from mental disorder" (Webster's Dictionary).

Free from mental disorder? Really?! My suspicion was confirmed. I was certain my dictionary had to be outdated so I turned to my computer. What is normal? I typed it in. And when I did there it was jumping out at me; "Cosmetic Psychopharmacology."

I immediately thought of the breast implants and liposuction I had in years prior. Those were considered cosmetic surgeries. Were they at all related? We are all familiar with the idea of cosmetic surgery but I wonder how many people think about the biggest reason we have them done? The honest truth, according to my research and that published in the Stanford Journal of Neuroscience, is that it's not because of some physical malady but because people want to enhance their physical appearance toward some aesthetic ideal. Sadly, I can't argue with their findings. I admit I'm guilty as charged.

I thought about how I had once looked to society for acceptance by comparing myself to the girls in school, in the magazines and on television. There were perfect bodies everywhere. I was well aware that in 1993, just about the time my generation was graduating from college, there seemed to be a huge increase in the number of cosmetic surgeries and prescriptions written for diet pills. More than likely, many of the bodies I compared myself to had some type of alteration, even the ones as far back as middle school, especially if we factored in air-brushing and computer enhancement to the equation. But somehow, in my mind at that time, that didn't matter. I felt compelled to relentlessly compare my own body to those perfect cosmetically re-touched masterpieces. So much so that in my quest for perfection, I had asked my parents for liposuction for my graduation present from nursing school.

Logic told me it was a false assessment to compare athletic performance with athletes who took steroids versus athletes who didn't, because obviously the group taking the drugs would more than likely have an unfair advantage. So why didn't my logic work the same way when it came to how I compared my body with others? Logic didn't seem to compute in this sense. Hence the poor choices I had made in the pursuit to become this thing called beautiful.

Cosmetic Psychopharmacology is the use of drugs to improve one's psychological condition in the absence of a clinical disorder. The term was first coined by Peter Kramer in 1993 in his bestseller *Listening to Prozac,* the same year I started taking the diet pills. Such use raises questions about what qualifies as a cosmetic use of psychoactive drugs and whether physicians prescribing psycho-pharmaceuticals for cosmetic purposes are acting within the boundaries of their proper role as physicians.

One in four Americans is currently taking a psychiatric medication. These drugs have the potential to be therapeutic. However, the sad reality is that current statistics indicate more people now than ever are taking prescription antidepressants, antianxiety, diet-pills and pain medications for periods of time that far exceed therapeutic recommendations from their health care providers. (In fact, four out of five antidepressant prescriptions are not even written by psychiatrists but by general practitioners, and more often than not, they're prescribed for patients without an actual diagnosis of depression, a John's Hopkins University study found.) And the problem is not just limited to antidepressants. With the alarming rate of non-specialists prescribing these and several other types of drugs, this is just the tip of the iceberg. What I found most terrifying is this diagnosis and type of medical treatment is not just limited to adults. An alarming number of children as young as kindergarten are being treated under this diagnosis.

I took a moment to ponder this information by allowing myself to investigate further all the possible medications that fall under this "label." In addition to antidepressants, there are antianxiety, anti-obesity, attention-deficit disorders, pain and hormone therapy medications to name a few. Could these be considered but not limited to falling under this category of Cosmetic Psychopharmacology? Absolutely.

I am confident that there are many incredible doctors out there, and I believe that there is a place for pharmacologic therapy, traditional and alternative medicine, and other treatment modalities that not only help to heal lives but end up saving lives. But my experience taught me to take responsibility by doing my part to seek first within for healing, considering non-pharmaceutical, non-invasive therapies, because I firmly believe there is healing within that cannot come from outside or man-made sources. How then do I first seek these things? The answer came to me – *Patience*. And perseverance.. We are living in a quick fix, instant gratification society so it's quite easy to get caught up and sucked into this way of thinking. Guilty again. Instant gratification can be a great thing, but when doing the work, I was instantly reminded that it would require patience, coupled with perseverance, determination and always being quiet and listening.

Using these tools, I would be able to access knowledge and wisdom. Through it I would find the answers I needed to heal. I also believe that there is a greater need in our society now more than ever to increase our knowledge and awareness of the way the entire body, mind and spirit communicate and work together to create healing. I finally realized if I was going to heal, to have the quality of life I felt I deserved, to be able to help my own children and others, I could no longer compromise. I had to stop putting all my hope in a medical system that wasn't addressing the entire person. My partnership with a medical system was imperative for my healing and the future healing of others. But I needed to align myself working only with a medical system that provided health care that included their mind and spirit, along with their brain and physical body.

I was certain there were intricate keys to achieving and maintaining total health and wellness for all humans and detoxing was one of them. In fact, I felt if we spent more time detoxing all parts of our body, mind and spirit on a regular basis, we would become healthier. I knew that detoxing was as individual as our blueprints, so it was essential I self-examine how I was living my life.

First, I needed to assess my intake of all of the things I was putting into my body and being exposed to. Then, I had examine my perceptions, feelings and behaviors towards myself, foods, exercise, sex, the environment, addictions, support systems, family, relationships, work and my connection with my creator. Next, it was essential that I had a clear understanding about the meaning of change. Change is a necessary part of life. Change can be exciting, empowering, awakening and beautiful. Change has the potential to bring with it the most wonderful, powerful and helpful advancements. However, the key is to have clarity on what exactly needs to change. In this fast-paced instant gratification world we live in, taking time to gain discernment with clarity and confidence can be most challenging because changing myself and being the change were two totally different things that would lend themselves to dramatically different results.

When something appears so right for others, how do I know if it's so right or wrong for me? To get this answer I had to take the time to get to know my unique blueprint, continued to seek the "right knowledge" for this blueprint and practice self-love, replacing judgment with assessment, using patience and forgiveness. Then, with this mental clarity, I could access what I needed to create the balance that would establish great health and wellness.

It was time for me to step up and put action to work. That meant I needed to start doing a better job contributing to my health by investing in my own capabilities because it was truly a partnership. The more I invested in myself, the less I felt I had to look to others for answers and support. Don't misunderstand me, consulting others and having their support can definitely be beneficial, which I am grateful for. But this was about demonstrating to myself that I was capable of making educated decisions for myself, all of which included my body, mind and spirit, with positive outcomes. In fact, the more equipped I would become. It opened the door for me to take an active role assisting the healthcare professional to determine the best plan of care for my body. Becoming a self-advocate would help me to facilitate and grow this partnership which would lead to empowerment for both parties. I thought about my children and understood that this entire process would affect them as well. Think about those airline flights many of us take with our families; if I couldn't put my own oxygen mask on first, how was I going to assist my children with theirs? Somehow, that thought fueled me with more determination than ever as I had a revelation – I wasn't doing all of this work just for my immediate benefit but doing this work for me would benefit my children and others as well. I remembered that knowledge is power, but at times there was so much information out there that it seemed quite easy to become overwhelmed at the thought of it, and often that makes it difficult for a person seeking knowledge to have clarity on just what route to go. Therefore at times like these unfortunately many of us throw our hands up and decide to rely on others to steer us in the right direction. That was how I felt and that is when I relied on the one thing I knew that worked – I made a call to the "Boss".

"Are you there God? It's me, Erica. I need your help. Please lead me only to the knowledge that is going to heal my body so that I may then take these tools with me, using them to help my children and to help others heal from needless suffering, too. If you want me to work for you, it's going to require that I get healthy first."

I typed in "hormonal imbalances, get healthy without drugs" and pressed enter.

Within a second or two, several medical conferences appeared on the screen. Immediately, I was drawn to a weeklong conference with classes offered in late March of 2012 in San Francisco, California. This was less than a month away and restricted to those in the healthcare industry. How convenient that I was a RN. I received a clear download to attend this conference.

Instantly, my mind raced, coming up with reasons not to go. Would I have a panic attack when I was there? How could I possibly retain the information in the classes when I was forgetting simple things? How would my family function without me for a week? What would Derek think?

*"Be quiet and listen,"* said the voice. *"Go."*

That's all I needed to hear. At once, my doubts and fear were replaced with determination and a quest for the knowledge and answers to all of my questions. A few weeks later, I found myself checking into The Westin St. Francis Hotel on Union Square.

"Welcome to the St. Francis, Mrs. McKenzie. Will your stay with us be for business or pleasure?" asked the desk clerk.

"Business."

"Wonderful!" And may I ask who you work for?" "God," I answered without hesitating. "I work for God." *I couldn't believe what I just said!* It babbled up right out of me. I was mortified.

"Well then, Mrs. McKenzie you've come to the right place. We need people like you here."

Staring dumbfounded at him, I smiled in relief. I had assumed he would react negatively. Once again, I received validation for remaining true to my authentic self and listening to God.

After wishing him a good evening, I was off to settle into my room. I was determined to get a good night's sleep because the conference started early the next morning.

Dressed and ready to go, I was beginning a new chapter in my life, one of healing and one that would give me the knowledge to help me finally become the much-needed advocate for my mind, body and spirit. I made my way over to the check-in table at a conference on health.

"Hello. Name please?" said the woman behind the registration table.

I looked into her beautiful blue eyes and my heart started pounding. Sweat beaded on my brow. My knees began to shake and I felt as though they were going to buckle.

*Oh no, God, not now. Please just let me check-in and take this class.* It didn't matter that I also felt like I was going to have diarrhea. I knew these physical symptoms all too well and I quickly acquiesced. I knew He had another assignment for me. *Ok, God, I'll do it, but you must give me the words to say. I'm letting go and it's in your hands.*

"Hello, I'm Erica McKenzie." I knelt down beside her, hoping I could whisper. It was hard enough to give a complete stranger a message and open myself to the possibility of a negative response, but I certainly didn't want the entire room to hear what I still considered *crazy talk.*

"I would like to share a message with you," I said. It just came bubbling out. "I would like to tell you that it's going to be ok. I know you are having a very hard time right now with your divorce. I know you have lost your way and you feel like you're completely alone, but I'm here to tell you that God has heard all of your cries to him. He is with you and everything is going to be better, I promise."

Her mouth dropped open and she gasped. Tears spilled freely from her eyes. Her co-worker, who was checking in people in the line next to us, turned to her and asked if she was ok.

The poor woman said, "No, I'm not okay! I have to take a break and talk to this woman right now."

She didn't give her co-worker a chance to respond, nor did she acknowledge the other people in line behind me. Instead, she leapt from her chair, took me by the arm and led me out the hallway into a small, unoccupied room.

She sat down. "I feel sick. How did you know what you just said about me? Do you know Bill?"

By this time all of the physical symptoms I was having completely subsided and I was feeling refreshed and energized.

"No, I don't know Bill. I don't know anything about you other than the message I just received for you."

"Well then, who gave you the message?"

"God," I said.

"How is that possible?"

"Well, I work for Him." *I can't believe I just said that again! How does this keep happening?* It's like I had no control over what comes out of my mouth. God has quite a sense of humor making me say that to everyone, but her response was completely unexpected.

She got very serious and said, "I can see it in your eyes. You do work for him. Everything you told me is true. I was just talking to God this morning because I received a nasty phone call from my ex and I just want everything to go away. I want to start over and be happy. I told God that I didn't think he's been listening to me because things seem so hopeless in my life. This divorce has been so stressful. I told him I didn't know if I had the strength to keep going.

"Normally, I look forward to these events but with everything I've been going through, I could hardly pull myself together this morning. I told God he *had* to help me. I came down the elevator, sat in my chair preparing to check people in for the conference, and there you were standing in my line. You delivered a message to me that you could not have known and I know God sent you in answer to my plea."

We sat for a while and I shared a few more personal messages in an effort to help her. From time to time, I still see her at conferences, she still thanks me, and I still remind her not to thank me but to thank God.

## My New Doctor

Attending that conference, I found an organization that was dedicated to educating healthcare professionals by providing continuing education, training, research, treatment modalities, protocols, and innovative diagnostic tools to aid in the implementation of effective longevity treatment. I spent three consecutive years traveling the country attending numerous medical conferences growing my knowledge with different organizations. I had the privilege of meeting several incredible doctors, one of whom became my new doctor.

When I met Dr. David Brownstein, words can't describe the joy I felt when he agreed to take me on as a patient. I attended my new patient visit with confidence, armed with the knowledge I had gained regarding my health issues. Throughout the visit the most amazing thing happened. As Dr. Brownstein performed a thorough health assessment, we engaged in an educated conversation, which included listening and participating for both parties. He performed extensive testing unlike any doctor had before. In fact, when I walked out of that patient visit, only two words could accurately describe how I felt, productive and empowered. When the results were in, he called me and said, "Erica, the first thing you must do is *detox*." Breathing a sigh of relief, I hung up the phone and began to cry, while laughing at the same time. Finally after all of these years, I told myself, I have found a doctor who understood the blueprint to achieving total wellness and healing of my body. I am thrilled to report Dr. Brownstein is still my doctor today and I am the healthiest I have been in twenty-five years!

ERICA MCKENZIE

# HEALTH IN THE SPIRIT

*"With God all things are possible."*

Matthew 19:26 (ESV)

After my NDE, I was still in the midst of raising my babies and trying to heal my body. I acknowledged that an important part of spiritual healing came through delivering messages. Frequently, I delivered messages to more than one person a day, and at times it was taxing and difficult. However, I had accepted that with the messages came numerous learning opportunities, one of which was understanding how to create the balance between my work in the spirit and the health of my body and mind. The physical symptoms I'd get when I was supposed to share a message were becoming very familiar to me.

At the same time, I often wondered if the person receiving these messages would judge me for sharing what I was compelled to. God taught me about judgment when I was in Heaven but at times, I still found the memories of the psych ward and the treatment I received if I talked about God flooded my mind, and I didn't feel safe.

I was definitely a work in progress and God could have easily said, *Erica we've already been over this in Heaven. How could you need more help than that?* But that wasn't the case. He was patient, kind and loving. Each time, I had those thoughts they were immediately squashed by an effective reminder from

Him to let go of the fear and stop operating in ego because it wasn't about me.

Withholding the messages caused me to feel physically ill and many times this manifested as a panic attack. If I withheld the message, it would completely drain my energy level to a point where I would be unable to function or accomplish the activities of daily living. When I let go of the fear, listened and shared the messages, I honored my God-given connection to Spirit and began to heal.

Sometimes necessary learning opportunities present themselves in what are considered a less-than-desirable fashion. For example, I noticed that around some people, I was allowed to see something about them generally no one else knew. Often, I was extremely drained just from walking past a certain person. It was as if they had unknowingly sucked the life force out of me. This was odd and very unsettling, yet eerily familiar. My mind would flood with the memories of when I was in Hell. Nonetheless, if I chose to reject fear, have faith and embrace it using my tools: my feelings, intuition and God's voice, I would gain knowledge, and that knowledge would become a powerful part of my healing.

During that time, when God said talk, I did. I didn't have a choice. There were times when I delivered messages to people and other times when I talked about my NDE. The instructions from God came through fast and furious. The grocery store, the gas station, and even the airport were no respite from sharing my experience and the messages downloaded to me for people, and yet it didn't matter because I understood that by letting Go and letting God, He was growing my gift exponentially. God was preparing me and I took it in stride and realized it was all part of my job for God.

## *Working for God*

On a recent trip home from a business meeting in 2014, I stood near a charging station at the gate waiting for my flight. I plugged in my new computer and heard someone say, "So how do you like your Surface Pro?"

I turned to find a very distinguished African American gentleman in his seventies waiting for my answer. We struck up a conversation when he mentioned that he also had one and had discovered a device to extend the battery life of his computer.

He directed me to a row of seats nearby and introduced me to his wife. I sat down. As he searched his pocket for the device, I suddenly felt dizzy and rooted to my chair. *Oh no. Here it goes again.* But seriously, these people would think I was nuts.

I swallowed hard and said, "I'm sorry. I just won't be able to pay attention to what you are saying about the battery until I share a message I have for you."

They both leaned in and waited for me to speak.

"I am supposed to tell you that God doesn't call the qualified, He qualifies the called."

His wife blurted out, "See! I told you she was an angel. I knew it!"

The man said, "You won't believe this. My wife and I were just at a convention in Detroit during the last few days for our congregation. We are ministers. We were learning how to listen and recognize signs from God. We really wanted to know if we were on the right path. I was the final speaker of the weekend and the last thing I said at the end of my speech in closing the conference was, *"God doesn't call the qualified; he qualifies the called."* You have no idea what hearing these words from you has meant to me. You have just validated exactly what we were learning this week."

I was so grateful that I was able to listen to God and have the courage once again to share a meaningful message with someone. It was not only validation for this couple; it was also validation for me of the importance of my faith and trust in God and His messages.

## *Premonitions*

While I was attending a medical conference in Orlando, Florida about bioidentical hormone replacement therapy, I found myself standing in a circle of physicians as my dear friend, Jim Paoletti, began the introductions. I shook each person's hand but stopped midway through my greeting with one particular person in the group. It was nothing I was surprised by at this point. Receiving downloads had become a normal occurrence, but this time it was the actual download itself that I was trying to process.

As I held his hand and looked into his eyes, a message for him came flooding to my mind.

"How is your mother?" I asked. He replied with a blank stare.

I continued, "It's been awhile since you've talked with her. I think your mom may not be well. You may want to reach out to her."

"I haven't spoken to my mother in fifteen years."

I reassured him. "It's going to be ok. Life is short. I think if you reach out to her this time things may be different. I feel that she doesn't have much time left here."

"How do you know?" he asked. "Do you know how much time she does have left?"

This is a common question for me and many times, I don't feel comfortable giving the answer. I've learned to rely on my power of discernment and allow God to guide me. In this particular case, this man was at a point in his journey that made this information necessary to help him rekindle a relationship with his mother in a timely fashion.

"Well, it's late Spring." I hesitated for a moment. "You don't have much time left. I think it's going to be early October of this year."

His face softened as his expression changed from surprise to concern. Over the following months, the doctor and I developed a wonderful friendship. He took my advice, reached out to his estranged mother, and rekindled their relationship. She passed away on October 2nd of that year.

It's still very difficult to stop a stranger and give them a message from God. These messages have become so strong after my near-death experience, that I become physically ill if I don't immediately stop and share the message that God has given me. I feel light-headed and nauseous and my body feels rooted to the ground as if I can't move. The minute I share the message, my symptoms vanish.

Rarely are the messages from a family member who has died; instead, many are messages to help heal a broken and hurting part of the person that I am contacting. Sometimes it's just a validation for the person when they've asked for a sign from God.

## Visitations

It's funny how God works. Recently, I was on the road with my good friend, Virginia. We stayed at John Sphar's house during my speaking engagement in San Jose, California. John is the leader of the San Jose Chapter of IANDS, the International Association of Near-Death Studies. Both Virginia and I noticed how cold our room was in comparison to the rest of the house.

When we returned later that evening, the temperature in the room had dropped so far that we both pulled on our sweatpants, sweatshirts and socks before climbing into bed. We didn't want to bother John, so we both continued to shiver from the drastic drop in temperature and waited to drift off to sleep. I awoke with a start in the middle of the night. Our room felt as if it were the temperature of a freezer. The smell of grapes permeated the air. I felt as if I'd been transported to another place. "Virginia, can you smell that?" I whispered. "It smells like grapes in here, like grape gum."

She mumbled, "What grapes? No, I can't smell any grapes. No, wait. I *do* smell grapes," she continued. "Shhh. Now go back to sleep."

I lay quietly in the dark with the very strong smell of grape gum around me until I eventually drifted off to sleep. We were both still sleeping when I received a text message early the next morning. I reached for my cell phone on the nightstand and checked the message. It was a mass text sent out by one of my high school classmates. Katie, the talented girl I mentioned in Chapter Three, had passed away the night before. I suddenly remembered the strong grape smell in the middle of the night and Kate's penchant for grape Hubba Bubba Bubble Gum. I know without a doubt that Katie had come to me that night to let me know that she was okay.

## Soul Separation

In May 2012, I boarded a flight to Kansas City returning from another medical conference. This time I was coming from Florida and I was looking forward to the first leg of the flight to Dallas. I'd never sat in first class before, but I had just befriended a pharmacist at this conference and we were booked for the same flight. He asked me to join him in first class so we could spend a few hours visiting. I didn't have the finances to upgrade my ticket so he suggested we just ask. I was astonished when the request was granted!

What an incredible way to end what had been a wonderful week of meeting medical professionals and learning new things. Once we became airborne, we had planned to talk about my

NDE, but God had other plans for me. My stomach clenched, my head started to spin and sweat began to roll from my forehead. *Oh dear God, please not on this flight.* I had just met this poor man at the medical conference and I rather enjoyed his company as he was like a walking medical encyclopedia. It most certainly was his gift and I was enjoying his company and I didn't want to freak him out.

My symptoms persisted. *What is it God? What do you want me to do?* I groaned aloud. The pain in my stomach was getting worse. I felt like I was going to have diarrhea and pass out at the same time.

The fasten seatbelt sign was still illuminated. I couldn't run to the lavatory. I was going to have to deal with it right there in that First Class seat. I closed my eyes in utter humiliation at what was going to happen next. *Dear God, you have my attention. What do you want me to do?*

"I'm sorry to have to ask for your help, Jim, but I'm not feeling so well. I need to go to the bathroom."

"The fasten seat belt sign is still on. Here, put these on and see if you can relax," he said handing me his Bose headphones.

My hands were shaking as I slipped them on. Jim held my hand in an effort to comfort me.

I thought to myself. *Relax Erica. Just relax.* But the feeling of losing control of my bodily functions from both ends was too great. I swallowed a big lump in my throat hoping to keep from vomiting.

"*Look,*" the voice said.

My eyes were instantly drawn to something out the airplane window. The classical music in the headphones faded. My hand felt as though it had let go of Jim's. I wasn't even sure if Jim was still there.

A strange yet familiar feeling returned. My spirit was leaving my physical body again. Where was I going now? As I began to panic, I realized there was nothing I could do but allow it all to unfold in front of me.

Outside the window in the clouds, a swirling pattern formed. It looked to be some sort of vortex, bright balls of luminous light with tails moving clockwise in a circle, like a miniature Ferris wheel. There were too many to count. I had no idea what they were, yet there was something so familiar about them. Just as that thought entered my mind, half of them stopped mid-motion and began to swirl counter-clockwise. Not one touched the other. The pattern seemed natural and effortless, yet I could feel there was some sort of propulsion to it. Strangely enough, I felt it calling to me. I mentally asked them to slow down just long enough so that I could study them. They heard my request and slowed so that I could take a closer look.

Suddenly, I realized what I was seeing. They were souls! They were the same kind of souls I saw in my NDE lifting off earth and effortlessly flying into Heaven. They were the silvery gold lights!

As soon as that thought of recognition entered my mind, they split apart and began to dance around on all of the clouds. It was a fantastic display of God's magnificence! I felt as though I was watching a production of the most incredible soul dancers.

Each was a different size. There were souls the size of pencil erasers, golf balls, softballs, volleyballs, basketballs and beach balls, and each of them had a tail. They were so ecstatic that I was able to see them and they began to communicate with me. I was downloaded with information along with a powerful, all-encompassing love such as I had felt in Heaven.

I'd long forgotten how lousy I felt. I had even forgotten about being on an airplane. *I was with my Heavenly family. I was home again!* As I continued to watch them, they ventured close to the airplane window and slowed their vibrational energy enough so that I could see their faces. These were people. My God! Tears spilled from my eyes. I knew them. I knew them all!

Basking in their love and knowledge, I continued to watch them. When they slowed enough for me to get a clear picture of their faces, their tails would fade. I don't know if the tails disappeared from existence or if it just faded to the point that I could no longer see them, but nonetheless, when they slowed to this point I observed every detail in their faces. They were a perfect sphere. They were three dimensional.

Like us, they had a frontal, side profile and posterior view. I had the knowledge that if I reached out to them I could join them. *I could fly.*

I knew how to do it. It felt as natural as blinking my eyes or taking a breath. It was what I did when I left my body for Heaven School each night following my NDE. I had no idea how long this went on and it didn't matter; my tears kept flowing. I was humbled by this beautiful experience. This was a gift from God.

*Thank you, God.* I knew that there was purpose in this gift and I was not going to take it for granted. Please God help me to remember, help me to understand, help me to know what it is that you wish for me to know. I work for you now, remember.

With that, I felt a squeeze on my hand. I was being pulled back. Another squeeze followed. Goosebumps exploded over my entire body. I was coming back into my human self and I couldn't stop it. In a daze, I glanced at my hand. Jim was still holding it.

"Are you O.K.? You're crying."

Tears barreled down my face. I pushed the headphones off my ears.

"Do you see them?" I asked.

"See what?"

"Look. Look there." I pointed out the window. My daze had quickly turned to excitement. "There they are!" I said. "I can see them! They're so beautiful!"

"Who are they? Tell me what you see."

My heart began to pound almost loud enough to hear it. I hesitated for a moment, but as I did, my less- than-desirable symptoms returned. I made a conscious effort to take a deep breath and with it, I turned to him and said, "I see the souls. I can see them."

Immediately the lesson for Jim began. I pointed as I described to him what I was seeing. The souls were playing. I wanted so desperately for him to be able to see what I was seeing, but somehow I knew he didn't need to see to believe and it was wonderful. I watched as they all came together again and constructed the Ferris-wheel-like pattern once again.

As the souls took their place in unison, they began to flow clockwise. As I watched, I could feel their vibration speed up. This created such a powerful force that it eventually came to a point where I could no longer see them, but I could feel them. They were still there and they were with me. They were a part of me and I was part of them.

Overcome with a deep sense of peace, my physical symptoms vanished. I was drained and weak. My head felt like it was in a fog. Somehow, I hadn't quite settled back into my body. As we prepared for landing, I wondered how I would manage to find my way to my next flight.

"I have a layover," Jim said. "Come with me to the flight club. I'll help you."

*Thank you, God*, I said silently. We deplaned and Jim helped me to a seat in the lounge. "I think I need to use the restroom."

Jim pulled me out my chair and helped me to my feet. "Let me help you to the restroom," he offered.

"It's O.K. Thank you, Jim. I'm feeling much better. It will do me good to walk."

The bathroom was no more than fifty feet away from our table. As I made my way from that chair to the bathroom, I began to visualize my hand reaching up well above my head and pulling myself, *my real self,* back down into my body. I knew this feeling of separation from my physical self. I had experienced it during my NDE. I am a spiritual being having a human experience, I thought, but I have to be able to function in this human body to carry out this experience.

It wasn't a painful feeling and I wasn't scared. I was able to feel the real me. I loved this free feeling of my higher self, yet I also loved the challenge of functioning inside my body too. I have to remind myself on occasion to pull myself back into my physical body. This was one of those times.

Over the years, I came to depend on this separation as a sign I was preparing to receive spiritual knowledge. This is how I separate each night to attend what I call Heaven School. Part of it was learning to smoothly rejoin my physical body afterward. Eventually, I made my way back to the table from the restroom. Jim was sitting there with a bewildered look on his face.

"Are you O.K.?" I asked.

He stared at me dumbfounded. "Are *you* ok?" he replied.

"Yes, I feel much, much better. I don't know what I would have done without your help. Thank you, again."

"Erica, when you were walking to the bathroom, I was so worried about you I wanted to make sure you didn't need me so I watched you walking away. Your feet weren't on the ground. You were floating!"

## *My New Relationship with Orbs*

Since the experience on the plane, I have seen these spirit balls of light daily. I learned that they are called orbs. The orbs join me several times a week when I walk and talk with God. They are as unique as we are. They are different sizes and colors and each have unique features, different levels of energies, messages and purpose. The love and positive energy I feel in their presence is contagious! When I see them, I look through the lenses of the glasses I brought back from Heaven. My eyes focus clearly now as I gaze upon the orbs and begin to study them. In their presence, I feel as though my brain unzips, leaving the weight of it off and my mind is finally free with no constraints, to work by itself. At once, it expands and I feel a rush of adrenalin accompanied by goosebumps from head to toe. My fingers reach up and begin to palpate the large soft spot on the top of my head to ensure my scalp is still intact. I am excited like a child who plays with their new Christmas gift. As it opens up, I am able to access depths of knowledge I have stored, yet normally can't figure out how to access. In this moment I feel like a genius, yet at the same time I feel as though I am a child again, thrilled by excitement and curiosity from head to toe. It feels like the best of both worlds.

These moments instantly became treasures because the way they made me feel emulates only a fraction of what I felt in Heaven – the real me but this time tapping into it while in my human physical body. Feeling this way caused me to long even more to return to my real home. I understand that's not possible, not yet anyway, as there is still more work to be done. But these experiences were glimpses that allowed me to see that my consciousness didn't have to be out of my physical body to access the bridge between Heaven and Earth. I didn't have to die either, I only had to be me. Not a rediscovered me, not a new and improved me, not even a want to be me, but a raw and real Erica.

As the months passed, the orbs began to join me in the car, in the stores and in my house. I quickly found that some of them had become regulars. Others, I would only see once or twice.

Everywhere I went the orbs would accompany me. Sometimes they came together in groups, sometimes they came alone, and sometimes they would join to form a variety of configurations. At times, they'd manifest into complete forms. Some were human, some were animals and some were neither human or animal. Telepathic communication with them came naturally. I found that as we communicated, I could invite them to come closer and they would even sit on my hand.

I especially enjoyed when this happened because I could examine their extraordinary intelligence and beauty. They weren't one-dimensional; instead, they were multidimensional and spherical. Many of them had human faces. It was as though the orb itself was a vehicle of sorts, a method of transportation if you will. I understood that the souls weren't contained by these orbs; it was just an extension of them. They were miraculous in all their splendor and I couldn't help but feel that I was witnessing a divine example of the bridge between Heaven and Earth.

It seemed the spherical shape allowed the spirit to gather a certain amount of energy that could be seen by humans and possibly also allowed them to travel. I noticed something else interesting. They appeared excited and vibrated faster when they congregated close to power lines. They also appeared unaffected by environmental factors or objects. I observed them in the snow, in the rain, and in the light and dark. I watched them pass through my hands, through pets, people, windows and cars.

They seemed to gravitate toward positive energy and situations where love was present. At my children's soccer games, I noticed several orbs hovering just above the player's heads. They seemed to be playing and having fun with the energy from the children.

Orbs also appeared at times when comfort was needed. Quite often, I witnessed them land on a person's cheek or go into their forehead, chest, or even into their mouth unaffected. What I witnessed brought no harm to the orb or to the host. Rather, it was an exchange and sharing of vibrational energy: a coming together to provide a method of communication in the form of love, support, understanding, healing and sometimes messages for that person. I felt strongly that this display of love carried powerful vibrations so strong that if measured against energy from power lines, the power lines would simply be unable to compete with the orbs.

My communication with them would quickly become a full-time job, as these encounters with orbs have become a daily event. I couldn't help but feel compelled to explore and push the boundaries of the knowledge I received from them. I realized they were always with me and the ability to see and interact with this phenomenon became another extension of me.

Recently, I was in Chicago visiting my sister. While there, I arranged to meet with a friend at one of the dog parks to share my experience with the orbs. He is a professional psychic, a genuine medium with an incredible gift from God for communicating with loved ones who have crossed. Matt Damon played him in the movie *Hereafter* which did a beautiful job of portraying his gift. But spending time with him at the dog park, I quickly appreciated that the movie had revealed just a fraction of his splendor.

We began to watch the people with their canines. You could feel the love exchange between the people and their pets. This love was a magnet for the orbs as they congregated in droves at the park. It was electrifying! I couldn't contain my excitement at the site of them. As I began to point out and describe to my friend what I was seeing, his answers gave confirmation to it. We began to take turns, each describing to the other the spectacular events that were unfolding in front of us. I was ecstatic but I had to remind myself to slow down, be quiet and listen to my friend and spirit as we did the work because this was a learning opportunity for me and I needed to embrace it. I loved the orbs but there are times when I have to function as a wife, mother and human being with minimal distraction. In the same manner, I find balance in my relationships on earth. I had to learn to find a balance between this world and the daily interaction with the Afterlife, and my friend was instrumental in guiding me with helpful suggestions.

"Thank you, God! Thank you so much for giving me the opportunity to participate in these lessons today as you have reminded me to fully access the potential of our gifts, remembering that we must use them in conjunction with each other. It is only when we come to the table with our unique selves, whether it's the business table, the relationship table, the dinner table, or even the dog park table that we empower each other. Working together, we can go on to do great things and today was a beautiful example."

Embracing our unique blueprints, we access our gifts and use the tools that are compatible to aid us on our missions. In my case, orbs are one of the many tools that I use. I am simply a vehicle, and I am filled with gratitude for my gifts. I remind myself it is by design that we use our gifts, not to just help ourselves, but to help others. I am extremely aware that if I choose to use my gifts in any other way, I will no longer be able to access them. It is with a humble heart I work with the Afterlife and others, and any knowledge gained I apply in an effort to be a light, to create a positive rippling effect for humanity.

# THE POWER TO HEAL

*"Be the change that you wish to see in the world."*

Mahatma Gandhi

t is up to us to be quiet and listen to be able to hear God's voice. It isn't always easy to receive these messages and do the inner work necessary to access our blueprints and grow our unique gifts. Sometimes it's difficult to believe in something that isn't tangible, but that's where faith comes in. God wouldn't have given us our unique blueprints and gifts, if He didn't also believe that we were capable of using them to the best of our ability.

But hand in hand with the gift of life goes the gift of free will. It is up to us to recognize, grow and utilize our blueprint and these gifts and then come together to help others. An important part of being able to access our blueprint, grow these gifts and heal is our ability to connect with our Creator. So a healthy body, mind and spirit is imperative. I struggled for many years with my health, but the more I became an advocate for my body, mind, and spirit, the stronger I was able to grow my gifts and heal my life. I realized one of my jobs is to serve by helping others recognize that their uniqueness is their value and their value is their contribution here on this earthly journey. If you are here on this planet, *you are valuable*. But recognizing that value can be most challenging at times especially in today's world when many of us are working hard to change our unique selves in desperation *to fit in.* In this fast-paced instant gratification society we live in, taking time to be quiet and listen to the right answers that are best for us, to gain discernment with clarity and confidence, can be most challenging. Therefore, the moment the thoughts begin to creep up causing us to lean towards changing ourselves, others or the world, I am reminded to stop, and ask myself these questions first:

*"I know I need to change something. However, is the something that I need to change really myself, or do I need to change the way I view myself compared with the rest of the world?"*

*"I know I want to change someone. However, is the someone that I want to change really that person, or do I need to change the way I view them compared with the rest of the world?"*

*"I know I want to change the world. However, what kind of place could the world be if instead, I became the change that I desire to see in the world?*

Please know that the future of mankind is nothing to be feared. We're simply on the next step, the next course of our humanity and it has the potential to be a positively incredible awakening experience. My purpose is to learn. My heart is to love. My boss is God and my work is to be *me.* I realize God gives us only what we can handle. It all makes sense now that God was preparing me for my new mission here on earth.

My near-death experience came with a responsibility and I take that responsibility seriously. I am devoted to applying what I learned through my near-death experience to myself and to others. My mission is to serve, as I step into my role as a nurse, healer and advocate devoted to sharing my NDE and lessons learned from my journey with as many people as I can. If any inspiration is seen through my story, I want to make it clear that I am only a rock. All that I am comes from my creator who I call God. This is not a 9-to-5 job. It is who I am 24/7 and I can't imagine doing anything else. Many people have asked me how I continue to have this remarkable passion and positive energy to work for God, advocate for others, and continue to deliver His messages and lessons; when inevitably there will be some who try to invalidate my experience and others who dismiss it because of a refusal to believe that what happened to me could be anything more than crazy?

*"Here's to the crazy ones. the misfits, the rebels, the troublemakers, the round pegs in the square holes...The ones who see things differently-they're not fond of rules...You can quote them, disagree with them, glorify or vilify them, but the only thing you can't do is ignore them because they change things...They push the human race forward, and while some may see them as the crazy ones, we see genius, because the ones who are crazy enough to think that they can change the world, are the ones who do. "*

*- Steve Jobs*

You may call me crazy but the answer is simple. I am a spiritual being who is having a human experience. I guess you could call it Earth school and I just have to say it... I fricken love this Earth School and this miracle called life! And I am so thankful for all of the opportunities that God has given me. God is Great! So I choose to help out of Love. And when my earthly mission is complete and I have the privilege to stand in God's presence once more, it is my hope to hear Him say, "Welcome home, Child. Job well done.

# COME TO THE TABLE

My near-death experience has helped me become the change that I would like to see in the world as I continue to learn and grow here on Earth School every day. It has inspired me to work passionately to help make our planet a better place for all by working hard to put action to my words. People have contacted me from all over the world asking for help on a multitude of topics. Many have graciously opened their hearts sharing their personal stories of spiritual awakening, spiritually transformative experiences, some grieving from loss, some are struggling to find their way, facing illness, bullying, personal struggles, relationship challenges, body-image issues, and some just trying to fit in.

The truth is, we all have a story and we all have questions. All of our stories and questions are important. And I am listening. So I created a table where everyone is welcome. Please visit www.ericamckenzie.com to further your own awakening or desire for healing your life, gaining knowledge or becoming a self-advocate, empowering yourself and helping others or to share your stories from your own personal journeys. There are many place-settings at this table. We are blessed to have experts from all over the country joining us to share their experiences, gifts and knowledge, addressing all topics from the Afterlife, medical health and wellness, to relationships, loss and issues like bullying and self-empowerment. In addition, I will feature experts sharing opportunities to volunteer and get involved, to offer service together with others. I will continue to listen, answer your questions, and provide valuable information and resources for all who are interested in these areas.

# DR. BROWNSTEIN'S
# CENTER OF HOLISTIC MEDICINE

My near-death experience inspired me to help make the world a better place for everyone, and Dr. David Brownstein's Holistic Medicine has made this possible. He is a God-send and I am so blessed to call him my doctor and friend. His expertise, dedication and knowledge has been instrumental in healing from all of my past health issues. I am so blessed to share that today because of him, I have been able to find my balance of health and wellness. Dr. Brownstein is a Board-Certified family physician and is one of the foremost practitioners of holistic medicine. He is the Medical Director of the Center for Holistic Medicine in West, Bloomfield, MI. He has lectured internationally to physicians and others about his success in using natural hormones and nutritional therapies in his practice. He is a graduate of the University of Michigan and Wayne State University School of Medicine. Dr. Brownstein has authored eleven life-healing books that illustrate the success he has had in treating many different conditions.

Dr. Brownstein's mission is to provide hope for those who are ill and to provide knowledge to help us all achieve our optimal health. I encourage each of you to please visit www.drbrownstein.com to further your own wellness awakening as you set forth increasing your knowledge and understanding of health in the body. You are on your way to becoming an empowered self-advocate, a priceless gift.

# ACKNOWLEDGMENTS

There is no doubt in my mind that I am the luckiest person in the world to have been blessed with my family. Each and every one of you have played a significant part in my life supporting me, loving me and not judging me. I know it hasn't been easy and has honestly been quite challenging to be a part of my life for years. Many of you have had to watch me suffer and lose my way and yet none of you have left my side. It is because of the love I feel from all of you that my book has become possible.

To Derek, my husband, we have been together for twenty-five years. I'm afraid it just might take me twenty-five more years to give back to you as much as you have given to me. You are a huge part of making this book possible, the same book I've been writing for twelve long years. Thank you for believing in me and thank you for loving all of me! There is no one I would rather continue to ride this fantastic rollercoaster of life with but you! You are the love of my life and there is no doubt that God had a plan when he brought us together. I love you!!!

To my children, Keenan, Ian and Kameron, this is where your mom gets all teary-eyed but of course this would come as no surprise to all of you. LOL. I can't thank each of you enough first for being the most incredible human beings! I really am the luckiest mom ever on this planet because you are all so loving and I want you to know as a parent I never imagined it possible that I would learn more about life and love from my own children than I have from each of you! I really appreciate how you have listened to me over the years because I know it hasn't been easy.

I've shared over and over how important it is to treat others with love, respect and kindness. I couldn't be more proud of how each of you have continued to demonstrate my request. It is the most important achievement there is.

You've been there through it all, my health challenges, the countless times you've had to witness your mom helping others, and all of the long days and nights year after year of me working on my book, videos and Web site in preparation for helping others with my message, often times instead of doing things with you. Thank you for loving, supporting, and sharing me with the world, all with patience, kindness and humor.

In addition, I want to thank my parents Wayne and Sue Lammel, my sister Sarah, my grandma Nonie, my Aunt Deb for your support and taking my author photo, and my Aunt Janet. Please know that I have always felt so loved from each of you and I would not be here today if it weren't for all of the support and encouragement you have given me.

My best friend Jennifer, if it weren't for you I'm quite certain I would have forgotten how to laugh. Thank you for forcing me to remember, always giving me wonderful memories as you have always made me feel loved for just being me.

I would like to thank Doug for helping to bring me life and loving me enough to let me go. A love that is a gift that only a parent can begin to understand.

A special thank you to my daughter Kameron McKenzie for volunteering to be the girl on my book cover – You mean the world to me.

To Dr. Rajiv Parti for believing in my message and giving so much of your time as you continue to dedicate yourself to collaborating with me as we continue to come together moving forward as we do this work for God.

My dear friends Virginia Hummel, Kenneth Ring, (a

pioneer in the Near-death community), Chris (Maxine), Tracy Simmons, Grandma Sherley Simmons, Jim Paoletti, Kori Simmons (the 1st teenager to read my story), all who donated hours of their time reading and helping to edit and critique my story and were most definitely the most loving positive cheerleaders, filling me full of encouragement and guidance.

To Bill Virga, Nadia McCaffrey, Sheri Lynn Martin, Drs. Pam Smith, Jack Monaco, for taking me under their wings, offering support and encouragement without wavering, supporting the importance of my message and my ability to help others. I have learned so much from each of you.

To PMH Atwater, Jeffery Long, and Pioneers to the NDE community for their passion to make this world a better place and seeing the valuable contribution this story brings to the table, and without hesitation endorsing me and my message.

To the most gracious media people ever, thank you – David Sunfellow, Bill Taylor, Lee Witting, host of NDE Radio, Sandra Champlain, host of the We Don't Die Radio show, The Tammi Baliszewski radio show, To clan mother Linda Jaquin the founder of the St. Louis NDE Retreat and to all my fellow fireflies, you are loved, and I appreciate you adopting me into your clan.

To my friend John Audette, (pioneer to the NDE community) co-founder of Eternea, thank you for your endorsement. Please visit www.eternea.org to further your knowledge of spiritually transformative experiences. Eternea also provides a valuable resource for scientists, academicians, researchers, theologians and members of the clergy who are interested in this field of study.

A Godsend, my dear Nadia McCaffrey a fellow Near-death experiencer and gold star mother & child experiencer with a life mission, founder of the Patrick McCaffrey Foundation.org, www.VeteransVillage.org.

To Martin of the Salt Lake City IANDS thank you for your support. To Jeff Olsen, you are a dear friend. Thank you for your support and bringing Joy to the table each time we work together. You are an incredible human being.

Since returning from my NDE in October 2002, I have been completely blessed with love and encouragement from thousands of amazing souls from all over the world. Every email, facebook message, conversation and letter has been such a gift to my heart as I have learned from each of you and has filled me with courage to continue to work hard to help others.

Last but certainly not least, to my most loyal family members...the one's that always agree with me and continue to teach me unconditional love each and every day my canine companions; Jessie, Chrisma, Trevor and Rex. Because of you guys the world most certainly is a much better place.

# ABOUT THE AUTHORS

**F**rom the first night that I was admitted to the psychiatric ward after sharing my near-death experience with my attending physician, God gave me clear instructions that I was to write my story down – all of it. Therefore, I did just that. I wish I could say along with God's instruction came this beautiful, flowing, easy-to-read story, but I can't.

I was thankful for the five years of journalism I had taken in college because it definitely helped me to become a better writer. However, it took thirteen long years to create the book in your hand and it is important to me to share why. I have difficulty learning and for years, I was ashamed and embarrassed by these challenges but more importantly, I looked at them as roadblocks.

I was never officially diagnosed with what many refer to as "learning disabilities" at the time I attended special classes in grade school, or had tutors throughout middle school, high school and college. It wasn't until after my NDE that I made the decision to never let a potential roadblock stand in my way again. No exceptions. So I did the "work" and finally sought the help of a medical professional and completed the necessary tests, resulting in a diagnosis of Dyslexia and Attention Deficit Disorder. Both made reading and writing especially challenging for me.

Over the years, I have spent countless hours writing my story to the best of my ability and I still couldn't manage to achieve the organizational flow necessary. What I needed was someone to help me who had the gift of writing and the ability to edit and organize my story.

God gives us all unique gifts. It was time for me to bring my gifts and uniqueness to the table with someone whose gifts could take my pages upon pages of writing, make sense of it, and assist me to create the order and flow of the story that follows. It had to remain in my words, even if that meant they appeared as frustratingly simple. I would not compromise and risk losing my voice or the importance of the messages that I was to share.

This person would also have to be able to keep up with all of the "downloads" that came to me during the writing process. This would be quite a challenge because many times downloads of information from Heaven came faster than I could articulate them.

Countless times, I tried to contact professional editors, writers, and book publishers in an effort to get the help I needed to finish this book. Each time I sent an email, made a phone call, or met someone in person, it appeared they were only interested in receiving my help and messages before they eventually cast me aside.

One particular evening, I felt unusually compelled to sit at my computer and work on my story. I closed my eyes and pleaded with God. "Please, please put someone into my life who will be quiet and listen to you when I ask them to help me. Let this person have a heart for you so that they won't judge or dismiss me. I have carried these messages for you, God, because I love you. You have been with me all these years. Only you have seen the countless number of times I've reached out in the effort to help others with love and compassion in my heart. I do it because I love you. Now I ask that you send someone to help me finish this book because you have shown me that I can't move forward on my mission until it is finished."

Two days later, I found myself on the phone with Virginia Hummel, creator of the Orb Whisperer website. Virginia asked me to share my near-death experience with her. She didn't know it, but it was her time to be quiet and listen to God. My story planted a seed in her heart, yet it would be up to her to nurture and grow it.

When I hung up the phone, God revealed to me that Virginia would be the person who would help me with my story. At the time, I couldn't see how that was possible. After all, she was "The Orb Whisperer," not "The Book Whisperer."

In the nearly two years since we met, Virginia and I have become great friends. My heart is filled with gratitude and love for this woman God put into my life. She has spent countless hours helping me with my story and patiently teaching me the tools that assisted me in removing my writing roadblocks, and all while in the midst of writing her own book on healing grief through spiritually transformative experiences after the death of her son. I am honored to say that I believe she is not only "The Orb Whisperer" but after collaborating with me to help write, organize, and edit my story, she is most certainly "The Book Whisperer" too.

**E R I C A   M C K E N Z I E** is an inspirational speaker, messenger, advocate, researcher and author. She is an active member of the National League for Nursing, American Nurses Association, The National Hospice and Palliative Organization, American Academy of Anti- Aging Medicine and the International Association for Near-Death Studies. She also serves on the board of Veteran's Village.

Erica is the mother of three high school teenagers. She is a near-death experiencer (NDE) determined to increase awareness by sharing her knowledge as she continues her research and collaborates with other experts in all areas of the Afterlife, NDE, medical health and wellness, self- esteem issues, and Hospice, along with human and animal rights issues.

She continues to demonstrate how we must work together to empower each other. She is a rock with a guiding light that radiates from within a beautiful demonstration of the Rippling Effect as she inspires people, helping them reconnect with our Divine Creator, identify and access our unique blueprint and gifts, and reminds us to truly love ourselves by helping see our value. And the best part is...she's just getting started!

For FAQs and to learn more about Erica's work, please visit her website: EricaMcKenzie.com.

ERICA MCKENZIE

VIRGINIA M. HUMMEL is the Chair of the Orb Encounters for Eternea.org, a global non-profit organization dedicated to the coalescence of science and spirituality, co-founded by Eben Alexander, M.D. and John Audette. She is an author, inspirational speaker and co-producer of a new documentary on healing grief through spiritually transformative experiences (STEs).

Virginia is the mother of four children and three grandchildren. With the death of her youngest son in 2006, Virginia experienced a series of spontaneous spiritual events, including the ability to see, interact and communicate with orbs, the spiritual phenomenon sweeping the globe. It was through this beautiful expression of Divine light she met Erica McKenzie.

She is the author of *Cracking the Grief Code: Healing Through Spiritually Transformative Experiences* and *Miracle Messenger: Signs From Above, Love from Beyond.*

Please visit her at VirginiaHummel.com devoted to healing for the enlightened soul (virginiahummel.com) and OrbWhisperer.com devoted to education and research of the Orb Phenomenon–The Divine light within each of us.

CPSIA information can be obtained
at www.ICGtesting.com
Printed in the USA
BVOW10s1958230717
489706BV00007B/81/P